The Letter and the Spirit

See www.lutheranvoices.com

The Letter and the Spirit

Discerning God's Will in a Complex World

David A. Brondos

Augsburg Fortress

Minneapolis

THE LETTER AND THE SPIRIT
Discerning God's Will in a Complex World

Scripture passages, unless otherwise marked, are from the New Revised Standard Version of the Bible, copyright © 1946, 1952, 1971, 1989 by the Division of Christian Education of the National Council of the Churches of Christ in the USA. Used by permission.

Scripture passages marked RSV are from the Revised Standard Version of the Bible, copyright © 1946, 1952, 1971, 1989 by the Division of Christian Education of the National Council of the Churches of Christ in the USA. Used by permission.

Direct translations by the author from the original languages are marked with an asterisk.

Editor: David Lott

Cover Design: © Koechel Peterson and Associates, Inc., Minneapolis, MN
www.koechelpeterson.com, and Diana Running; Cover photo: © Ablestock.com.

Brondos, David A, 1958-
    The letter and the Spirit : discerning God's will in a complex world / David A. Brondos.
        p. cm.—(Lutheran voices)
    ISBN 0-8066-4935-6 (pbk. : alk. paper)
    1. Ethics in the Bible. 2. Christian ethics—Biblical teaching. 3. Bible—Criticism, interpretation, etc. 4. God—Will. 5. Divine commands (Ethics) 6. Christian ethics—Lutheran authors. I. Title. II. Series.

    BS680.E84B76 2005
    241'.0441—dc22   2005013801

Manufactured in the U.S.A.

09   08   07   06   05   1   2   3   4   5   6   7   8   9   10

Contents

Acknowledgments

This book grew out of a paper presented several years ago at a Biblical Symposium on "Communities in Crisis" at the Evangelical Theological Seminary in Matanzas, Cuba, and later published by the Seminary under the title "Libertad, Letra y Espíritu en la Interpretación Bíblica" ("Freedom, Letter and Spirit in Biblical Interpretation"), together with the other papers from the Symposium. In 2003 I rewrote the article in English, and shared it with Mark Allan Powell, the Robert and Phyllis Leatherman Professor of New Testament at Trinity Lutheran Seminary in Columbus, Ohio. Mark was kind enough to share his reactions with me and pass the article on to Tim Huffman, the John H. F. Kuder Professor of Christian Mission at Trinity and editor of the *Trinity Seminary Review*. An abridged version of the article, titled "Freedom, the 'Letter' and the 'Spirit': Interpreting Scripture with the 'Mind of Christ'", appeared in the Winter/Spring 2005 volume of that journal. At the suggestion of Michael West, editor-in-chief at Fortress Press, I decided to develop the material from the two articles into a book proposal for the *Lutheran Voices* series. Since then, it has been wonderful working on the project with Scott Tunseth and the rest of the people at Augsburg Fortress (particularly Abby Coles, David Lott, and Michelle L. N. Cook), all of whom have been extremely helpful. Thanks also to Mark Powell, who took time out from his busy schedule to review the manuscript and offer his suggestions and assistance. To all of these people, I am deeply grateful.

Of course, in various ways I have also depended on the support of many other people, including the staff of the Division for Global Mission of the ELCA, my bishop the Rev. Floyd Schoenhals, the administration and faculty of the Theological Community of Mexico, my fellow pastors and members of the Lutheran Church of the Good Shepherd in Mexico City, and most of all my wife, Alicia, and daughters, Elizabeth and Monica Julie. In addition to expressing my profound gratitude to all of them, however, I would especially like to thank my students at the Theological Community of Mexico. They have been my dialogue partners in developing the ideas presented in this book, which owes a great deal to their insights, encouragement, inspiration, and friendship.

David A. Brondos

Introduction

With tears in her eyes and pain etched across her face, Carmen poured out to me her feelings of immense grief over her recent divorce. She had come to church the previous Sunday and had asked to meet with me during the week. After almost thirty years of marriage, her husband had left her for another woman, and the divorce had been finalized only a few weeks earlier. Yet her reason for coming was not so much to receive pastoral counseling, as to ask if she could take communion at our church, even though she was not Lutheran. In her own church, the priest had told her that because she was now divorced, she was no longer allowed to commune, since Jesus had prohibited divorce. Receiving the Lord's Supper, she explained to me, meant more to her than anyone could imagine, and she was desperately looking for a church that would allow her to commune.

On another occasion, a young man named Fernando came to me with a question not unlike Carmen's. After attending our church for several Sundays, he had invited me to lunch so that we might talk. Fernando confided to me that he knew from a young age that he was homosexual and had struggled a great deal with the problems this raised for him, having been raised in a devout Christian family. When he sought counseling from his own pastor on the subject, he had been told that the Bible strictly condemned homosexuality as sinful and that he would no longer be welcome in the church unless he repented. For several years, Fernando had undergone counseling elsewhere, but despite his efforts to change, he continued to experience the same feelings. While he had been sexually abstinent, he was considering entering into a committed relationship with another man, but first wanted to know whether he would be welcome at our church and at the Lord's Table if he did.

Marcos, a doctor working with AIDS patients, sought counseling regarding a young married couple, both of whom were HIV-positive. They had been cautioned that it was not advisable for them to have children, but in spite of their precautions, the wife had become pregnant. Marcos told me that the couple was agonizing over the question of whether she should have an abortion. As a doctor, he felt an abortion was recommendable considering the risks involved, but as a Christian, he had always been told that abortion involved taking an innocent life. What was he to tell this couple?

A young woman named Isabel had decided that she wished to enroll at the Lutheran seminary in Mexico City, but had deep doubts about whether she should seek to become a pastor. The church body of which her congregation was a part did not allow women to be ordained into the pastoral ministry, claiming that in a number of his epistles Paul assigns a subordinate role to women in both home and church and prohibits them from exercising authority over men. While Isabel felt God was calling her to the pastoral ministry, she did not know how to respond to what seemed to be strong biblical arguments prohibiting women from serving as pastors.

Faithful to our belief that in the Holy Scriptures we have the inspired word of God, as Christians we look to those Scriptures for guidance in the many difficult decisions that we face in life, both as individuals and as a church. According to Lutheran teaching, there is no human authority above Scripture. In fact, we insist that "Scripture interprets Scripture." This means that Scripture itself teaches us how we are to interpret it, providing us with the guidelines and principles we need to understand what it says. We look at each particular passage of Scripture in the light of the teachings of Scripture as a whole. On this basis, we reject the claim that only certain persons or groups of people are able to interpret Scripture correctly, a claim that would end up making *them* the supreme authority, rather than Scripture itself. On many issues, the Bible seems to speak quite clearly, commanding certain things and prohibiting others. Other contemporary issues, however, are not directly addressed there: nowhere in Scripture, for example, do we find discussions concerning abortion, euthanasia, birth control, or human cloning.

While it is perhaps no surprise that Christians disagree on many of these questions that are not specifically considered in Scripture, the fact that some churches (such as the Evangelical Lutheran Church in America) are open to discussing and accepting certain things that Scripture seems clearly to prohibit represents a scandal for many Christians, especially those of a more conservative or fundamentalist background. How can we accept divorce and remarriage, not only among lay people but clergy as well, given the fact that Jesus says explicitly that to divorce one's spouse and marry another person constitutes adultery? Why do we have women in leadership roles in the church, not only as pastors but also as bishops, if Paul says that they are to be submissive and not exercise authority over men? Why do we not simply condemn the practice of abortion when God's law commands, "You shall not kill"? And how can we as Lutherans even *consider* the question of whether or not to bless homosexual unions and accept gay and lesbian people into the pastoral ministry when the Bible appears to condemn homosexuality in no uncertain terms?

In the following pages, we will examine the way in which we look to Scripture for guidance in dealing with questions like these, both as a church and as individuals and families. Our purpose is not so much to propose specific answers to such questions as it is to examine *how* we should address them on the basis of Scripture. What is involved is learning to read and interpret Scripture in ways that are faithful to Scripture itself as we seek to discern God's will for our lives and those of others.

Questions for reflection and discussion

1. What do you consider to be some of the most important ethical issues facing us as a church and as a society today? What perspectives do you have on those issues?

2. What difficult ethical decisions have you or those close to you had to make? How have you looked to Scripture for guidance in making those decisions?

1

Keeping the Commandments in Ancient Jewish Thought

"Remember the sabbath day, to keep it holy." "Honor your father and your mother." "You shall not kill." "You shall not commit adultery." Commandments such as these seem simple and straightforward. It doesn't take a PhD in theology or biblical studies to be able to understand them or to figure out when they are being obeyed or disobeyed. Or does it?

The need for interpretation

In Jesus' day, keeping the commandments was of the utmost importance for faithful Jews, who believed that they had been chosen by God to be God's special covenant people. The commandments to be fulfilled were not just the ten that most Christians usually associate with the Law of Moses, but *all* of the commandments contained in the first five books of the Bible, or the "Torah," as it is called in Judaism. In fact, the Jewish rabbis actually claimed to count 613 commandments in the Torah, of which 248 were positive and the other 365 negative, expressing prohibitions.

These commandments had to do with many different aspects of life, including prayer, health and hygiene, the administration of justice, relations in family and society, business practices, and the treatment of slaves and animals. A considerable number prescribed the way God was to be worshiped in the Jerusalem Temple, particularly through the sacrificial offerings presented by the priests; participation

1

in the Jewish festivals was also mandated. Others had to do with questions of diet: certain foods were defined as "clean" (*kosher* in Hebrew), while others were unclean and thus not to be eaten, such as pork. One of the commandments given even before Moses' time was the commandment to circumcise all male children. To be a faithful Jew meant observing *all* of these commandments.

Yet defining precisely *how* they were to be observed was not always easy. An obvious example is the sabbath commandment, which prescribes that no work be done on the seventh day of the week, or *shabbath*, which means "rest" in Hebrew. Yet precisely what constituted work? Could one, for example, prepare something to eat or drink for oneself, or make a meal for others? Was it permissible to heat food or drink, or was it necessary to eat everything at room temperature? If something spilled or broke on the floor, could it be cleaned up? Could one write, and if so, how much writing was allowed before it might be considered work? What objects could one lift or carry without breaking the commandment? If one wanted to go visit friends or family, how far could one walk on the sabbath? And precisely when did the sabbath day begin and end? In order to keep the sabbath faithfully, it was necessary to provide answers to questions such as these.

The same problems of interpretation arise with regard to other commandments. Who ultimately defined precisely what constituted honoring or dishonoring one's parents? In certain circumstances, such as waging war, executing justice, and combating idolatry (as Phinehas did in Numbers 25), the commandment not to kill was not in force; but exactly what circumstances justified the taking of another's life? Was it permissible to kill in self-defense, for instance, or if someone was breaking into your home (see Exod. 22:2-3)? In order that the poor might find something to eat, the Law prescribed that the edges of the fields were not to be reaped when the crops were harvested, and the vineyards were not to be stripped bare (Lev. 19:9-10). But precisely how far from the edge might one harvest, and what percentage of the grapes was to be left on the vine? The Law also stated that one had to lend to the poor (Deut. 15:7-11); but did one really have to lend money to every poor person requesting it? How much was one obliged to lend? And who qualified as "poor" so as to have the right to eat from the unharvested grain or demand a loan?

Differences in interpretation

Examples such as these make it clear that, in order to observe the commandments, it was necessary first to interpret them. But who was to carry out this task? It is not surprising that a variety of interpretations arose, sometimes at odds with each other. Two of the most important schools of interpretation in the first century were led by the Jewish teachers Hillel and Shammai, the latter of whom was stricter on most points. For example, the school or house of Shammai differed from the house of Hillel with regard to what constituted grounds for divorce, and interpreted the sabbath law as prohibiting giving alms for the poor in the synagogue and praying for the sick on that day, while the house of Hillel allowed for these things. Although both schools agreed that under certain conditions one might pick up a pot from the stove or move a ladder on the sabbath, the school of Hillel permitted one to put the pot or ladder back where it had been, while the school of Shammai regarded this as a violation of the sabbath commandment.[1]

In spite of the many differences among the various schools and teachers of the Law, eventually a tradition of interpretation arose in Judaism with regard to the commandments, so that there was a great deal of agreement regarding how most of them were to be kept. For example, it was generally agreed that the distance that one could walk on the sabbath was two thousand cubits, or about half a mile. We find reference to this tradition in the New Testament, where Luke refers to "a sabbath day's journey" in Acts 1:12, supposing that everyone knew precisely what that distance was. This Jewish tradition of interpretation already existed in oral form in Jesus' day, and was also beginning to take shape in written form. Eventually, much of this tradition was gathered together in Jewish writings such as the Mishnah and the Talmud, completed in about 200 and 400 C.E. respectively, which Jewish people still study today in order to interpret the commandments.

Of course, by Jesus' day, there was also another reason why teachers and experts in the Law were necessary: the Torah had been written in ancient Hebrew, a language that most Jews no longer could understand well, if at all. Most of those in Palestine spoke Aramaic, which is similar to Hebrew, while those living outside of Palestine spoke Greek or a number of other languages. Thus, observance of the commandments was only possible thanks to the work of scholars who translated and interpreted those commandments for other Jews.

The Law as God's eternal will for Israel

For many Christians today, the discussions we find in the Jewish tradition concerning the minutest details of the observance of the commandments might seem trite, trivial, or even ridiculous. Did it really matter whether or not one put a pot back on the stove or moved a ladder on the sabbath? In Jewish thought, however, keeping the commandments was of utmost importance; out of all the nations of the earth, God had chosen only one, Israel, as God's special people and had given the Law to them alone so that it might be observed. By obeying the commandments, the Jewish people would remain in the covenant God had established with them and continue to be God's "treasured possession out of all the peoples" and a "holy nation" (Exod. 19:5-6). In passages such as Deuteronomy 7:12-14 and 28:1-14, God had told the people of Israel that their receiving an abundance of blessings depended on their being obedient to all the commandments they were being given. Therefore, the people needed lines to be drawn for them indicating how to observe faithfully each and every commandment. For this reason, in Jewish thought, discussions regarding matters such as the precise manner in which to observe the sabbath were anything but trivial. Indeed, they were of great importance, because the people would be in danger of forfeiting the blessings God had promised to them in the covenant if they were not diligent in keeping the commandments in every detail.

In fact, many Jews held the commandments of the Mosaic Law in such high esteem that they eventually came to affirm that the Torah had existed before creation and was the instrument with which the world had been created: "The world and the fullness thereof were created only for the sake of the Torah."[2] According to biblical scholar Werner Foerster, there is evidence that by the end of the first century C.E. many Jews believed that the Torah was eternal and would be observed even in the future age of redemption: "[T]he Torah is from all eternity and for all eternity the valid will of God. . . . The creation of the world is intended to provide a sphere in which God's will (= Torah) will be done."[3] In fact, in the Law itself it is stated that the people were not to add anything to what God had commanded, nor take anything away (Deut. 4:2), and that many of the commandments were "perpetual ordinances" that every generation of Israelites was to observe (see, for example, Exod. 12:17 and 31:16). This meant that for Jews the commandments of the Torah applied to all times and places; in that sense, they transcended history. While God had given the Law to the people in a specific historical context under Moses, the Law itself had not been designed for that particular context alone, but for every context in which they might find themselves.

Of course, even though the commandments were considered to be valid always and everywhere for Jews, their interpretation obviously might need to change from one context to another. For example, one commandment prescribed that men and women were not to wear clothing of the opposite sex (Deut. 22:5); yet what men and women wore varied considerably from time to time and place to place. In one ancient Jewish writing this commandment was interpreted to mean that a woman was not to wear white clothes and men were not to put on colored garments.[4] Obviously, this responds to a particular historical context, and Jews in other contexts probably would not have interpreted this commandment in the same way.

In fact, in certain times and places, some of the commandments could simply no longer be observed. When there was no Temple, such as during the Babylonian exile and after the Temple's destruction by the Romans in 70 C.E., observing the commandments regarding worship and sacrifice was impossible. Jews who lived outside of Palestine could not be expected to observe many of the laws having to do with questions related to the land, because other laws applied in those places. Furthermore, as new conditions arose over the centuries due to cultural, political, social, and technological developments, it was necessary to find ways to apply the commandments to situations that had never been contemplated at the time when the Law was originally given. Yet while the contexts in which the commandments were to be interpreted and applied undoubtedly changed a great deal over the centuries, in Jewish thought the commandments themselves did not. They were inalterable, and had been given by God once and for all to be obeyed by the Jewish people of all generations.

The commandments and *shalom* for all

Why had God given the commandments to Israel? What was the purpose of the Torah? A close look at the Law of Moses reveals that for the most part it fulfills the same purpose that human laws in general are designed to fulfill: namely, the establishment of justice, equity, and well-being in society. Numerous passages of the Torah state this purpose explicitly: God tells the children of Israel to obey the Law so that "it may go well with you and with your children after

you for ever," and that "you may prosper in all that you do" (Deut. 12:28, 29:9 RSV). Obedience to the Law would bring abundant blessings upon the people, not only because God would shower those blessings on them from above, but because obedience to the commandments in and of itself would have beneficial consequences for them. "There will be justice for us, if we are careful to do all this commandment before the LORD our God" (Deut. 6:25*).

The many blessings promised by God to the people might be summed up in a single Hebrew word, *shalom*. In Leviticus 26:6, for example, the Israelites are told that if they keep the commandments, God will grant "*shalom* in the land." Usually we translate *shalom* into English as "peace." As the Old Testament scholar George Knight observed years ago, however, *shalom* means much more than that: "The verbal root from which it derives conveys the conception of being whole or being complete or sound; consequently the transitive form of the verb *shalam* means to make whole, to restore, to complete." *Shalom* thus involves a total well-being in body, mind and soul, abundance, prosperity, material security, tranquillity, contentment, "the right relations which can ideally obtain amongst men [and women] living together in harmony," "fulness of life, harmony, satisfaction, completion, integrity—all these English words together are required to express the Hebrew noun—both in [a people's] communal life and in the life of individual men and women."[5]

The concept of justice should be understood against this same background. In fact, we can define justice as "*shalom* for *all*." That is, justice exists when everyone in society enjoys wholeness and well-being in body, mind, and soul, having all that they need. For this reason, in Hebrew thought, justice was often equated with mercy and compassion, rather than being its opposite. This idea is clear in many passages from the Psalms (see, for example, 89:14, 103:6–8, 145:17), as it is in Isaiah 30:18: "Therefore the LORD waits to be gracious to you; therefore he will rise up to show mercy to you. For the LORD is a God of justice." To do justice or to judge is an act of kindness, mercy, and salvation in biblical thought, because it involves acting to establish *shalom* for those who suffer oppression or are in need.

For this reason, the fact that God comes to "judge" or do justice, or sends judges or kings to do so, is cause for great rejoicing: the heavens, earth, and sea, together with all that is in them, rejoice and sing because the Lord is coming to "judge the world with justice" (Ps. 96:10-13*). In many of these passages (including Deut. 6:25), the Hebrew word *tsedaqah,* often translated "righteousness," actually should be translated "justice," just as the Hebrew adjective *tsaddīq* should often be translated as "just" rather than "righteous."

Close consideration of the commandments found in the Torah makes it clear that many of them had precisely this purpose of seeking to ensure justice and *shalom* for everyone in the society. Any society will be better off when murder, adultery, stealing, false witness, and coveting are prohibited, as the Ten Commandments prescribe (Exod. 20:2-17). Laws such as the requirement to quarantine those with a contagious disease such as leprosy (Leviticus 13–14), as well as many of the commandments regarding diet and hygiene, were no doubt intended primarily to contribute to the people's physical health and avoid illness in their midst. The prohibition of sexual promiscuity and violence, adultery, prostitution, incest, or even "uncovering the nakedness" of others that might lead to illicit sexual relations (Lev. 18:6-20, 19:29, 20:10-21; Deut. 22:13-30, 23:17), as well as the command to honor one's parents, were clearly aimed at protecting, strengthening, and preserving the family. The sabbath command was given to all of the people so that everyone, including the slaves and the animals, might rest and be refreshed (Deut. 5:12-14). A man who had recently been married, planted a vineyard, or bought a home was not to go to war for a year so that he might not die before enjoying these things (Deut. 20:5-7). The book of

Deuteronomy even commands the people to "rejoice" before God in all of their undertakings (Deut. 12:18).

Other commandments sought to establish justice by avoiding oppression and maintaining a level of equity among the people. Many laws protected those most subject to abuse, such as foreigners, widows, the handicapped, orphans, and the poor. The Jubilee laws (Lev. 25, Deut. 15) were an attempt to avoid a situation in which some might grow too rich and powerful in relation to others. By canceling debts, freeing slaves every seven years, and having the land and other possessions given back to their previous owners, the uneven distribution of wealth and power could be avoided: "there will be no poor among you" (Deut. 15:4 RSV). Slaves were not to be oppressed, but treated well, and workers were to be paid on the same day they had labored (Deut. 24:14-15); balances and weights were to be just (Lev. 19:35-36). Justice would also be brought about by a judicial system that was fair and equitable to all. Corruption and bribery were to be avoided, and measures were to be taken to ensure that the weaker elements of society would not be trampled upon (Lev. 19:15; Deut. 1:16-17, 16:18-20, 27:19).

Not only were the people commanded not to oppress or take advantage of one another; they were also told to love one another, care for those in need, refrain from taking revenge or bearing grudges, and even help their enemies: "you shall love your neighbor as yourself" (Lev. 19:18; see also 19:17; Exod. 23:4-5). As Old Testament scholar Georg Fohrer notes, "Thus help for the weak and oppressed that could not be defined in legal terms was also included."[6] That is, the well-being of all could only be attained through concrete acts of love and compassion for those in need that went beyond legal obligations. These commandments defined what it meant to love God with all one's heart, soul, and might (Deut. 6:5); to love God did not merely involve some sentimental response toward God, but an active obedience and unswerving commitment to doing God's will as it was made explicit in the commandments.

Of course, the Law also prescribed certain penalties, even execution, in the case of certain offenses. Yet the purpose of these penalties was believed to be positive, since they were considered necessary in order to observe and enforce the laws and to uphold justice. Even the so-called "talion principle," which demands an eye for an eye and a tooth for a tooth (Exod. 21:23-25), held a positive purpose. Rather than prescribing or justifying acts of revenge, since it applied only in a court of law, it sought to ensure that the retribution prescribed by the court was proportional to the damage inflicted (one tooth for a tooth), and neither excessive (two teeth for a tooth) nor unjustly lenient (no teeth for a tooth). This commandment was not applied literally, but was used as a principle to ensure equity.

The Law as God's gracious gift

Precisely because obedience to the commandments of the Law was to result in justice and *shalom* for Israel, the Jewish people have always considered the Law to be a tremendous blessing. The word *torah* actually means "guidance" or "instruction"; the Law was thus a gracious gift given to Israel by God, since it pointed out to them the way to live. God had given them the commandments for their own good (Deut. 10:13). As the writer of Psalm 119 expresses, the Law was thus a source of great joy: "I will delight in your statutes. . . . Your law is my delight. . . . Oh, how I love your law! . . . Great peace [*shalom*] have those who love your law . . ." (Ps. 119:16, 77, 97, 165).

Nevertheless, the Law would only serve as a blessing if it fulfilled its purpose. At times, although the people of Israel observed many of the commandments, they failed to practice justice and concern for those in need as God had prescribed. When this happened, the prophets of Israel spoke out. The book of Isaiah, for example, begins with God sternly reproaching the people: they were observing faithfully the commandments prescribing sacrificial offerings, prayers, new moons, and festivals, but were nevertheless oppressing the poor. Therefore, they are told that God does not want their sacrifices and will refuse to listen to their prayers until they change their ways: "cease to do evil, learn to do good; seek justice, rescue the oppressed, defend the orphan, plead for the widow" (Isa. 1:16-17). Similarly, the prophet Amos cries out against those who "trample on the needy, and bring to ruin the poor of the land," breaking God's law even when they observed the festivals (Amos 8:4-6).

In the minds of the prophets, then, true observance of the commandments involved practicing justice and opposing all forms of oppression and evil. This was stressed, not only by the prophets, but also by Jewish teachers from ancient times up to the present: ultimately, what God really requires of all is "to do justice, and to love kindness, and to walk humbly with your God" (Micah 6:8). In love, God had given Israel the commandments so that the justice and *shalom* proclaimed by the prophets might become a reality for all.

Questions for reflection and discussion

1. How has this chapter changed your perspective on the Old Testament Law and on Judaism?

2. Read one or more of the following chapters from the Torah and reflect on what you read in the light of what we have seen here regarding the purpose of the Law: Exodus 21; Exodus 22; Leviticus 19; Deuteronomy 24.

3. Reflect on the understanding of justice as "*shalom* for *all*." Is that how you have traditionally understood the notion of justice? How is it commonly understood in our society today?

4. Read Amos 2:4-8, 5:21-24, and 8:4-6. What is the prophet Amos saying about the relationship between observance of the Law and justice?

2

Jesus' Interpretation of the Law

"Why are you doing what is not lawful on the sabbath?" "Why do your disciples break the tradition of the elders?" "This man is not from God, for he does not observe the sabbath." According to all four Gospels, conflicts frequently arose between Jesus and a number of his Jewish opponents over questions regarding the observance of the commandments of the Mosaic Law, as is evident from these passages (Luke 6:2, Matt. 15:2, John 9:16).

How did Jesus interpret the Law of Moses, and why was his interpretation so controversial in the eyes of many other Jews? Both Jewish and Christian scholars have debated these questions among themselves extensively in recent years. While these scholars have differences of opinion on many points, nevertheless there is widespread agreement amongst them on some of the more basic elements of Jesus' interpretation of the Law.[1]

Conflict with the scribes and Pharisees

The Gospel according to Mark presents Jesus' ministry as generating conflict almost from the very start. In the second chapter, Jesus upsets some of the scribes and Pharisees by forgiving the sins of a paralyzed man (2:1-12), calling a tax collector to follow him, and then dining with tax collectors and "sinners" (2:13-17). While questions related to the observance of the Law of Moses no doubt had something to do with the adverse reaction of Jesus' opponents in these stories, not until the end of chapter 2 and beginning of

chapter 3 do they openly accuse Jesus of breaking the Law and teaching others to do the same. There we read in Mark 2:23—3:6:

> One sabbath [Jesus] was going through the grainfields; and as they made their way his disciples began to pluck heads of grain. The Pharisees said to him, "Look, why are they doing what is not lawful on the sabbath?" And he said to them, "Have you never read what David did when he and his companions were hungry and in need of food? He entered the house of God, when Abiathar was high priest, and ate the bread of the Presence, which it is not lawful for any but the priests to eat, and he gave some to his companions." Then he said to them, "The sabbath was made for humankind, and not humankind for the sabbath; so the Son of Man is lord even of the sabbath."
>
> Again he entered the synagogue, and a man was there who had a withered hand. They watched him to see whether he would cure him on the sabbath, so that they might accuse him. And he said to the man who had the withered hand, "Come forward." Then he said to them, "Is it lawful to do good or to do harm on the sabbath, to save life or to kill?" But they were silent. He looked around at them with anger; he was grieved at their hardness of heart and said to the man, "Stretch out your hand." He stretched it out, and his hand was restored. The Pharisees went out and immediately conspired with the Herodians against him, how to destroy him.

Before examining this passage more closely, it is important to note who these Pharisees are, as well as the scribes appearing earlier in Mark 2. The Pharisees, one of several religious parties or groups existing in Jesus' day, had already been in existence for over one hundred fifty years before his birth. While there is considerable debate regarding the extent of their power and influence at the time of Jesus' ministry, it seems clear that their primary concern was with

the proper interpretation of the Law, as well as its precise observance, both by themselves and others.[2] In fact, it is widely accepted
that there was a direct link between the Pharisees and the rabbis or
teachers of the Law that we encounter in the Mishnah and Talmud,
who focused their attention on discussing questions such as those
noted at the outset of chapter 1.

What is important for us to note here, however, is that we must
not assume that the Pharisees and scribes who are described as being
in constant conflict with Jesus were representative of Jews as a
whole. In fact, it is likely that they were not even representative of
the Pharisees and scribes in general. There were many different
interpretations of the Law, as noted in chapter 1. Evidently, the religious leaders who took offense at some of Jesus' actions tended to be
more on the conservative or strict side, as the school of Shammai
was. They may have been only a small group of influential individuals, particularly since there may not have been many Pharisees in
Galilee. Almost any group of people has some individuals who tend
to act like the Pharisees and scribes who entered into conflict with
Jesus (in fact, you might even have a few of them in your own congregation!). At any rate, not all Pharisees and scribes were hypocrites
and mean-spirited, oppressive individuals like the ones who oppose
Jesus throughout the Gospels. In fact, the Gospels and Acts indicate
that some of the Pharisees and religious leaders were friendly with
Jesus and supportive of him, and even came to be his followers (see
Luke 13:31, 23:50; John 3:1; Acts 15:5, 23:6).

Plucking grain on the sabbath

In the first of these two stories, the Pharisees point out that, by
plucking grain and eating it, Jesus' disciples are doing something
that is forbidden on the sabbath. Of course, from our perspective
today, it might seem strange to claim that picking a few grains of
wheat and eating them constituted work; after all, they were not
picking any large quantities.

Interestingly, however, Jesus does not argue with the Pharisees over that question. Instead, he concedes that what the disciples were doing was not lawful, by pointing out that David also did something that was not lawful when he and his companions were hungry. The Mosaic Law prescribed laying out the "bread of the Presence" or "showbread" on a special table in the Holy Place of the tabernacle (later the Temple) as an offering to God. This bread was to be changed every Sabbath, and the priests were to eat the old loaves there in the Holy Place (Exod. 25:30, Lev. 24:5-9). No one else was allowed to eat of this bread, but when David was fleeing from Saul, he asked the priest Ahimelech, Abiathar's father, to give him five loaves for him and his men so that they might satisfy their hunger, and Ahimelech obliged (1 Sam 21:1-6, 2 Sam. 8:17). Jesus' argument here, then, seems fairly clear: when there is an urgency regarding a basic human need, such as the need for food, it is permissible to violate a commandment of God in order to satisfy that need, as David did. Therefore, it was acceptable for his disciples to do the same.

Jesus then goes on to add, "The sabbath was made for humankind, and not humankind for the sabbath." As noted in chapter 1, some Jews held the view that God had made the world for the Torah, which existed previous to creation. In other words, God had brought the world into existence to be a place where the commandments of the Torah might be observed. Such a view is similar to the claim that human beings were made for the sabbath law, as if the law itself had precedence over human beings. In that case, what God cared about most was that human beings obey the commandments for their own good.

Jesus rejects the idea that human beings were made for the sabbath, and instead insists that the sabbath was given for the sake of human beings. What ultimately concerns God is not so much that the Law be kept, but that human needs be met; in fact, this was the concern that had led God to give the Law in the first place. As

noted in chapter 1, the purpose of the sabbath had been to contribute to human well-being by prescribing rest for human beings,
so that they might not be overworked and might enjoy life. Thus,
for Jesus, precisely because God had given the sabbath commandment and the other commandments to satisfy human needs, those
commandments might be set aside when, instead of serving to *meet*
human needs, they *prevented* human beings from satisfying those
needs, such as the need to eat. In this case, the *purpose* for which
God had given the commandment was being fulfilled, even though
the commandment itself was being broken.

Healing on the sabbath

In the second part of the passage cited above, the person violating the Law is Jesus himself rather than his disciples, according to
his opponents. In their opinion, to heal on the sabbath violated the
commandment to rest. Here again, according to our definition of
the term today, what Jesus did would not appear to constitute
"work." One must remember, however, that medical practices in
those days were in many ways different from ours, and that in
essence what Jesus was doing was giving a medical consultation, as
a doctor or healer would do in ancient times. It is also important to
note that this was no medical emergency; the man's paralyzed hand
was not putting his life or health at risk, and his condition was not
going to grow worse in one day. Thus there was no need to attend
to him on the sabbath; it could wait until the next day.

When Jesus senses the need to defend his actions, he asks those
opposing him, "Is it lawful to do good or to do harm on the sabbath,
to save life or to kill?" This question provides us with an excellent
insight into Jesus' interpretation of the Law, since it has to do with
the *purpose* of the sabbath commandment. Literally, the sabbath
commandment as it appears in the Hebrew Scriptures prescribes
neither doing good nor harm, and neither saving life nor killing; it
simply prescribes rest. In Jesus' mind, however, because the sabbath

commandment was given to promote human wholeness and well-being, it actually prescribed doing good and saving life.

It would be helpful to introduce here the distinction that is commonly made between the *letter* and the *spirit* of the Law: the *letter* has to do with what is literally stated in a commandment, while the *spirit* has to do with the *purpose* or *intent* behind a commandment. According to Jesus' opponents in this story, Jesus was sinning because he was violating the *letter* of the commandment, which prescribed that no work be done on the sabbath, such as giving medical treatment when there was no urgent reason to do so. According to Jesus, however, *he* was the one keeping the sabbath, because he was fulfilling the *purpose* of the sabbath by doing good and restoring a person to fullness of life. It was his opponents who were actually standing in violation of the sabbath commandment, because for them adhering to the *letter* of the commandment was more important than fulfilling its *spirit*. In fact, Mark even presents Jesus as getting angry at his opponents for wanting to prohibit him from helping the man on the basis of the Law, since that seemed to give the Law precedence over human well-being.

Nevertheless, while from our perspective today it is easy to criticize those who opposed Jesus, it is important to understand their point of view as well. Although they would have agreed with the notion that God had given the Law for the purpose of promoting human well-being, they would have insisted that precisely because of that purpose, it was necessary to be very strict about literal observance of the Law. Once one starts bending rules, making unnecessary exceptions, and being lax about what God commands, it is not long before the commandment is no longer respected and obeyed, and therefore it can no longer fulfill its purpose. If people are going to start plucking a little grain and giving nonemergency medical attention on the sabbath, pretty soon more and more people will be plucking more and more grain, and the doctors and healers will be just as busy on the sabbath as they are during the rest of the week. Then the whole point of having a day of rest will be lost. For them, to violate the letter of the Law inevitably involved violating its spirit as well.

In response to this, it should be noted that Jesus does not abolish the letter of the Law, saying that one can do whatever one wants on the sabbath as long as one has good intentions and can argue that it is for a good purpose. This comes out even more clearly in Matthew's account of this story, where Jesus tells his opponents, "Suppose one of you has only one sheep and it falls into a pit on the sabbath; will you not lay hold of it and lift it out? How much more valuable is a human being than a sheep! So it is lawful to do good on the sabbath" (Matt. 12:11-12). Jesus here seems to be appealing to the Jewish belief that the Torah commands humane treatment of animals; as the Talmud later stated, "Avoiding making animals suffer is a Torah obligation" (*Bava Metzi'a* 32b).

In effect, then, there are two laws in question: one prescribing rest, and the other prescribing alleviating the suffering of animals. Jesus appeals to the second one, saying that this overrides the first, so as to argue that if alleviating animal suffering overrides the sabbath commandment, the same must be even more true with regard to alleviating human suffering. Thus his action is justified, not just on the basis of the Law's spirit, but its letter as well. We see the same principle in Jesus' justification of his disciples picking grain on the sabbath in Matthew's version, where Jesus points out that "on the sabbath the priests in the temple break the sabbath and yet are guiltless" (Matt. 12:5). Here again, there are two conflicting commandments: the one prescribing rest on the sabbath, and the one prescribing that priests present sacrifices even on the sabbath, which overrides the first.

In Matthew's Gospel, therefore, Jesus appeals to the letter of the Law itself to justify his actions and those of his disciples. At the root of the conflict, therefore, is not merely a literal versus a spiritual interpretation of the Law, but an interpretation where concern for human wholeness is secondary versus an interpretation where that concern overrides others. This principle is itself found in the Law, which commands, "you shall love your neighbor as yourself" (Lev. 19:18). In fact, Jesus is presented as quoting Hosea 6:6 as well in this context, which says that God desires "mercy and not sacrifice" (Matt. 12:7). The idea is that, to be faithful to the Law, principles such as mercy and kindness must be at the heart of any interpretation of its commandments.

Other conflict stories

The Gospels of Luke and John report that Jesus healed on the sabbath on several other occasions and continued to face opposition from certain Pharisees and other religious leaders for doing so (see Luke 13:10-17, 14:1-6; John 5:1-18, 7:21-24, 9:1-41). The principle involved in most of these cases is essentially the same: since the purpose of the sabbath and the Law in general is to contribute to human wholeness, in Jesus' mind he was being faithful to that Law when healing others, rather than violating it.

The Evangelists report conflicts between Jesus and the Jewish religious leaders over other questions as well. In Mark 7, some of the Pharisees and scribes criticize Jesus for allowing his disciples to eat without washing their hands, thus breaking "the tradition of the elders" (vv. 1-5). Jesus responds (vv. 6-8) by accusing them of honoring God with their lips but not their hearts and of teaching human precepts as divine doctrines, citing Isaiah 29:13. For Jesus, the type of Judaism represented by his opponents had given rise to many traditions of interpretation that were not faithful to the commandments, apparently since they gave priority to things other than human well-being.

Immediately Jesus cites an example of this. After quoting the commandment to honor one's father and mother, he points out that their tradition allowed grown children to take the money destined for the support of their elderly parents and instead dedicate it to God by spending it on sacrificial offerings and gifts to God (vv. 9-13). At that time, of course, parents depended a great deal on their children, since there was no Social Security or retirement program in place. In this way, Jesus' opponents violated the commandment to care for one's parents, justifying their actions on the basis of their tradition, which supposedly honored God.

Jesus then goes on to tell those around him that "there is nothing outside a person that by going in can defile, but the things that come out are what defile" (vv. 14-15). Once alone with his disciples, he explains his words to them: what matters most is not the food that one eats, or whether that food is eaten with hands that are washed, but the words and actions that come out of a person. "For it is from within, from the human heart, that evil intentions come: fornication, theft, murder, adultery, avarice, wickedness, deceit, licentiousness, envy, slander, pride, folly. All these evil things come from within, and they defile a person" (vv. 21-23).

Mark comments that when Jesus taught that what goes into a person does not make him or her impure, "he declared all foods clean," that is, "kosher." While this appears to be Mark's later interpretation of Jesus' words rather than something stated explicitly by Jesus himself, what is involved is the laying aside of the dietary regulations concerning clean and unclean foods found in the Mosaic Law. The idea is that these regulations no longer matter; rather, what matters is that one avoid practicing evil and injustice in relation to others. This is what constitutes true purity.

Elsewhere, Jesus levels similar criticisms against the Pharisees and scribes: they "tithe mint, dill, and cummin, and have neglected the weightier matters of the law: justice and mercy and faith" (Matt. 23:23). This involves fulfilling the letter of the Law while neglecting its spirit, although the letter must still be observed as well. "They tie up heavy burdens, hard to bear, and lay them on the shoulders of others," and "lock people out of the kingdom of heaven" through their teaching and practices that claim to be faithful to the Law (Matt. 23:4, 13). "They devour widows' houses and for the sake of appearance say long prayers" (Mark 12:40), and "clean the outside of the cup and of the dish," but on the inside "are full of greed and wickedness" (Luke 11:39).

The same implicit criticism of religious leaders is found in Jesus' parable of the Good Samaritan, where the priest and Levite refuse to help the man left half-dead by thieves (Luke 10:30-37). Jesus' actions against the money-changers and the vendors at the Jerusalem Temple may also have been a protest against the corruption and injustices of the religious authorities, who used the system of worship ordained by the Mosaic Law to their own personal benefit (Luke 19:45-46).[3]

Jesus' teaching on the Law

Several other passages from the Gospels give us insight into Jesus' interpretation of the Law. Perhaps the most important of these is found in Matthew 5 in the Sermon on the Mount. There Jesus insists that he has come to fulfill the Law and Prophets, rather than abolishing them, and stresses the need to fulfill the letter of the Law (vv. 17-19). He then goes on to teach that literal fulfillment of the commandments is insufficient. One must refrain not only from murder, but also from becoming angry with others or insulting them (vv. 21-22). The commandment not to commit adultery also prohibits a man from looking at a woman with lust in his heart (vv. 27-28). For Jesus, true fulfillment of these and all the other commandments involves doing good to others (including one's enemies) and desiring their well-being, refraining from seeing others as objects to be used for one's own pleasure or interests, avoiding actions that might harm others unjustly, and being concerned about what is just, right, and merciful.

Elsewhere, we find Jesus' teaching on divorce (Matt. 5:31-32, 19:3-9). According to the Torah (Deut. 24:1-4), a man could present his wife with a certificate of divorce and send her away simply because he found something objectionable about her. Jesus rejects this commandment, saying that it had been given due to the "hardness of heart" of men such as his opponents, and teaches that "anyone who divorces his wife, except on the ground of unchastity, causes her to commit adultery."

It is important to note the context in which Jesus spoke these words. This law gave a right and privilege to men that women did not have; thus, a man could put away his wife for any reason and she would be left on her own. Some scholars have argued that Jesus' concern here was that women not be left without any support, in which case they would need to find someone else willing to care for them and perhaps marry them; others have insisted that this was not the case, since the wife would be left with sufficient resources.[4] In any case, it is clear that Jesus' rejection of men putting away their wives for whatever reason so as to remarry, and perhaps make it necessary for the woman to remarry as well, arises out of his concern for justice and human well-being. Spouses are to love each other and care for each other.

Jesus' concern for the spirit of the Law is evident in several other passages as well. When asked to summarize the Law, Jesus cites from the Torah the command to love God with all of one's being (Deut. 6:5), but derives from this a second commandment, taken from the Torah as well: "you shall love your neighbor as yourself" (Matt. 22:34-40; see Lev. 19:18). When the rich young man tells Jesus that he has kept all of the commandments ever since he was young, Jesus tells him to sell all that he has, give it to the poor, and follow him (Mark 10:17-22). This implies that, although the young man may have observed the letter of the commandments, he was still far from keeping their spirit. And in John's Gospel, Jesus tells his disciples that he is giving them a "new commandment," which is that they love one another (John 13:34; 15:12, 17). By observing the spirit of the Law and not merely its letter, Jesus' disciples would have a righteousness that "exceeds that of the scribes and Pharisees" (Matt. 5:20).

It is clear, then, that for Jesus what the Law ultimately commands is seeking justice and *shalom* for all; in this regard, his teaching is in continuity with what we find in both the Law and the Prophets, as well as ancient Judaism. Yet his stress on the spirit of the Law led to positions that were more radical than those of his opponents. At times, they believed he was violating or at least showing disrespect for the Law, whereas Jesus believed that he was fulfilling it, because he was being faithful to its purpose or intent. For Jesus, those who were in reality violating the Law were those who cared only about the letter of the Law and disregarded its spirit, applying it in ways that brought injustice, suffering, and oppression into the lives of others.

Questions for reflection and discussion

1. Why do you think the Pharisees and scribes responded as they did to Jesus' actions? What were they ultimately concerned about? Where do we see that kind of thinking today in our church and society?

2. Examine some of the laws in our society today in light of the "spirit–letter" distinction, attempting to discern the "spirit" of each law so as to see how it is intended to contribute in some way to human well-being.

3. Some people argue, as the Pharisees and scribes did regarding plucking grain and healing on the sabbath, that to keep the spirit of the law we must be very strict about insisting on the observance of the letter. How do you evaluate such an argument?

4. Read Matthew 23:1-4, 13-15, and 23-39. Reflect on the reasons for Jesus' anger in light of his concern for justice and *shalom* for all. What does verse 37 have to say about Jesus' motivation for speaking out so strongly against his adversaries?

3

Jesus' Ministry of Wholeness

Unlike many of the Jewish religious leaders of his day, Jesus' teaching and ministry did not revolve around questions having to do with the Mosaic Law. Biblical scholar E. P. Sanders has noted that Jesus "did not say to potential followers, 'Study with me six hours each week, and within six years I shall teach you the true interpretation of the law.'"[1] Jesus never established his own school for studying and interpreting the Law, as many of the rabbis did. In fact, when Jesus discusses questions related to the Law in the Gospels, usually it is in reaction or response to those who raise legal issues with him, rather than something done at his own initiative.

If the Law was not of primary importance to Jesus, then what was? The Gospels provide a clear answer to this question: Jesus dedicated himself to reaching out to others to bring healing and *shalom* into their lives, and called and prepared others as his followers to do the same.

Jesus as above the Law

In light of Jesus' insistence that he came "not to abolish but to fulfill" the Law and the Prophets (Matt. 5:17-18), it is surprising that he often appears to have little interest in questions of the Law, and at times even shows disregard for it. As noted in chapter 2, Jesus questioned what the Law taught regarding divorce, and perhaps the distinction between clean and unclean food as well. For many Jews, this would be seen as placing himself not only above the Law, but above Moses, since it implied that he had the authority to set aside or alter the divine commandments given through Moses.[2]

This same claim comes across implicitly in the teaching attributed to Jesus in the Sermon on the Mount, where he repeats on several occasions, "You have heard that it was said," and then after mentioning some commandment or precept, adds, "But *I* say to you." In ancient Judaism, the use of the passive voice in speaking was one way to avoid using God's name. Thus, "it was said" would be understood as referring to what God had said through Moses. For Jesus, therefore, to mention what God had commanded in the Law, and then add, "But *I* say to you," would sound offensive to many Jews, as if Jesus were above the Law and perhaps even adding to it, as Deuteronomy 4:2 prohibits. It is not difficult to imagine the reaction of most Christians today if some preacher were to use a similar formula in a sermon: "You have heard that in the Gospels Jesus said . . . ; but *I* say to you . . ."

In the stories that tell of the conflicts regarding observance of the sabbath, on a couple of occasions Jesus is presented as stating explicitly his superiority over the Law. After telling his opponents that "the sabbath was made for humankind, and not humankind for the sabbath," he continues, "the Son of Man is lord even of the sabbath" (Mark 2:27-28). In Matthew's account of the same story, after Jesus notes that "the priests in the temple break the sabbath and yet are guiltless," he says, "I tell you, something greater than the temple is here" (Matt. 12:5-6). This implies that what Jesus was doing was in some way superior to what took place at the Temple, the holiest place in Judaism, where God was believed to dwell.

Some New Testament scholars have argued that the controversy over Jesus' forgiving sins must be understood against this same background.[3] In Jewish thought, God alone could forgive sins, as Jesus' opponents state when he tells the paralytic that his sins are forgiven (Mark 2:5-8). Of course, God had given authority to the priests to forgive sins as well; it had been prescribed in the Law that those who needed forgiveness and cleansing from impurity were to follow the rituals laid out there, making the necessary offerings at the

Temple. But when Jesus forgave sins, he appeared to be setting aside the procedure laid out by God in the Law and appropriating to himself the authority from God to do so.

In fact, in the Gospels we find certain language used of Jesus that was commonly used in Judaism with regard to the Torah.[4] Whereas in Judaism it was common to speak of taking on the "yoke of the Law," Jesus instead called on others to take on *his* yoke, and promised that he himself would give them what the sabbath commandment was intended to provide, namely, rest (Matt. 11:28-29). Instead of affirming that the words of the Law were eternal and would never pass away, Jesus says, "Heaven and earth will pass away, but *my words* will not pass away" (Matt. 24:35). While some Jews believed that the Torah existed before creation, and that all things had been made for the Torah, in John's Gospel it is said that Jesus existed before all things as God's Word, and that everything came into being through him (John 1:1-3). And throughout his ministry, instead of calling on others to follow the Law more carefully, as many of the Jewish leaders did, Jesus called on others to *follow him,* regarding this as more important.

Jesus as bringer of wholeness

If Jesus was regarded as being in some way superior to the Law and above it, then he must have been seen as bringing something that the Law could not offer. And if the Law was intended to be God's instrument for giving wholeness, well-being, and justice to God's people, then the idea must have been that these things are found in greater measure in Jesus. This claim seems to be at the root of much of what we read in the Gospels, where Jesus heals the sick, casts out demons, miraculously feeds the hungry, and even raises the dead to life. Whereas the Law *excluded* from the community people like lepers and women with chronic hemorrhages, declaring them impure and prohibiting all physical contact with them, Jesus touched them so as to heal them and restore them to wholeness, thereby enabling them to live fully as members of God's people once again. He thus did things that the Law could never do.[5]

Above all, Jesus' ministry was one of *compassion*. Matthew mentions Jesus' compassion for the multitudes in the context of his teaching, preaching, and healing activity (9:35-36), while Mark states that this same compassion for the multitude moved Jesus to teach them (6:34). Likewise, his motivation for feeding the five thousand and the four thousand is said to have been his compassion for those he taught and healed (Matt. 14:14-21, 15:32-38). Other passages also speak of Jesus being moved to mercy upon encountering those in need (Matt. 20:34, Mark 1:41, Luke 7:13).

As we saw in the last chapter, not only were things such as mercy, compassion, and love at the heart of Jesus' interpretation of the commandments, but he also insisted that these things took precedence over anything the Law commanded. What mattered most was reaching out to others to bring wholeness and healing into their lives. For this reason, Jesus constantly was in fellowship with people who were regarded by many of the more religious Jews as sinners and impure, such as tax collectors and sinful women; in that culture, eating with people involved openly accepting them as one's friends, and thus approving of them. For this, Jesus faced a great deal of criticism. When asked why he ate with such people, Jesus responded by saying that he had "come to call not the righteous but sinners," and telling his opponents, "Go and learn what this means, 'I desire mercy, not sacrifice'" (Matt. 9:10-13). These last words from Hosea 6:6 once again stress that Jesus believed he was being faithful to the prophets, who demanded justice and mercy rather than mere observance of the commandments (such as those prescribing sacrificial offerings). Perhaps for this reason Jesus generally speaks of fulfilling, not only the *Law*, but the Law *and the Prophets* (Matt. 5:17, 7:12, 22:40); to truly fulfill the commandments involved being concerned about mercy and compassion, as the prophets consistently taught.

Of course, for the scribes and Pharisees who opposed Jesus, it was acceptable to have fellowship with such people, provided that they first fulfill the condition of repentance, changing their way of life so as to begin to obey the Law. For Jesus merely to accept them as they were, in their sinful condition, communicated the idea that keeping the commandments did not matter. Yet in the Gospels we do not find Jesus refusing to eat and drink with those considered "sinners" until they had first fulfilled the condition of repentance. He never tells anyone, "First you must change your way of life, and then I will accept you and eat with you." On the contrary, he ate with those such as Zacchaeus and accepted expressions of affection from people such as the sinful woman who washed his feet with her tears and anointed them with oil in the house of Simon the Pharisee. In the former case, while Zacchaeus decided to give away much of what he had obtained (probably illicitly) to those in need, and to give back four times the amount of anything of which he had defrauded anyone, this was not because Jesus told him to do so. Rather, it was a reaction to the fact that Jesus had first accepted him freely and graciously (Luke 19:1-10). In the case of the sinful woman, Jesus forgave her sins without asking her first to repent and change her way of life, though her tears might be taken as a sign of remorse (Luke 7:36-50). Jesus also is said to have taught that the tax collectors and prostitutes would go ahead of many of the religious leaders into the kingdom of God (Matt. 21:31), and to have told the parables of the lost coin, the lost sheep, and the prodigal son in response to the complaint that he welcomed sinners and ate with them (Luke 15:1-32).

Of course, in order to have *shalom* in the present, it is necessary to have hope for the future. In proclaiming the coming reign of God, and claiming that that reign would come in its fullness through him, Jesus gave others a ground for hope. His proclamation of the gospel and the reign of God was therefore an integral part of his work to make others whole. Jesus often defined his ministry in terms of "saving" others, referring both to their being healed from their maladies and to the coming of God's reign. It is interesting to note that the Greek word for salvation (*sōtēria*) used in the Gospels is originally derived from an adjective (*sōs*), which literally meant "whole" or "sound." This wholeness is what Jesus had come to bring in the present and what he promised to bring in the future as well.

For Jesus, then, making people whole did not merely involve healing them from their illnesses and resolving their problems, but showing them unconditional love, mercy, and grace, as well as giving them hope for the future. All of this was something that the Law could never do.

The authority of Jesus' disciples

Not only did Jesus himself seek to bring healing and wholeness into the lives of others; he also prepared disciples and sent them out to carry out the same ministry. Luke says that "Jesus called the twelve together and gave them power and authority over all demons and to cure diseases, and he sent them out to proclaim the kingdom of God and to heal" (Luke 9:1-2); subsequently, another seventy disciples were appointed and sent out (Luke 10:1). After his resurrection, Jesus sends the disciples out once more. Matthew's Gospel ends with Jesus claiming to have all power and authority and telling his disciples to go and make disciples of all nations, baptizing and teaching them; he also promises to be with them always (Matt. 28:18-20). In the Book of Acts, Luke presents the risen Jesus promising to pour out the Holy Spirit upon the disciples so that they might be his witnesses "in Jerusalem, in all Judea and Samaria, and to the ends of the earth" (Acts 1:8). And in John's Gospel, Jesus tells the disciples on the day of his resurrection, "As the Father has sent me, so I send you" (John 20:21). They were thus to go out to do the ministry for which he had prepared them.

According to Matthew, Jesus gave his disciples authority not only to heal, cast out demons, teach, and baptize, but also to "bind and loose." After giving Peter such authority (Matt. 16:19), Jesus grants the same authority to all of his disciples: "Truly I tell you, whatever you bind on earth will be bound in heaven, and whatever you loose on earth will be loosed in heaven" (Matt. 18:18). Interestingly, the only time Jesus mentions the "church" explicitly in the Gospels is in the context of these two passages (Matt. 16:18, 18:17).

Some New Testament scholars have pointed out that the language of "binding and loosing" has its roots in Judaism, where the rabbis determined whether or not certain commandments applied to specific situations; a commandment might be "bound" as applicable, or "loosed" as not applicable, depending on the context.[6] In effect, Jesus was giving his disciples the authority to determine what was acceptable behavior and what was not; whatever decisions they made in this regard "on earth" would be respected "in heaven," that is, by God. This meant that they could insist on the fulfillment of the letter of the Law or set it aside if they considered it necessary to accomplish their mission, and thus were not bound by the Law in deciding ethical questions, although no doubt they were to be guided by it.

A similar idea appears in John's Gospel. After appearing to his disciples on the day of his resurrection and sending them out, as we just noted, Jesus "breathed on them and said to them, 'Receive the Holy Spirit. If you forgive the sins of any, they are forgiven them; if you retain the sins of any, they are retained'" (John 20:22-23). Just as the disciples are given the authority to "bind and loose" in Matthew's Gospel, here they are given the authority to declare what actions are forgivable and unforgivable among those belonging to the community of Jesus' followers.

In this last passage, the authority to forgive or retain sins is tied to the disciples' reception of the Holy Spirit. This implies that the Holy Spirit will guide them in determining what is or is not acceptable. Previously in the Gospel of John, Jesus had told his disciples that the Holy Spirit would teach them everything and remind them of all that he had said (John 14:26). Subsequently, Jesus had said to them, "I still have many things to say to you, but you cannot bear them now. When the Spirit of truth comes, he will guide you into all the truth" (John 16:12-13). The idea here is that Jesus still has more things to say to his disciples, but he will not do so until after his resurrection and glorification; then he will continue to speak to them by means of the Holy Spirit. Furthermore, when Jesus says here that the Holy Spirit will "teach" and "guide" the disciples, he is ascribing to the Spirit the same function that the Torah had in Judaism; as noted in chapter 1, *torah* literally means "instruction" or "guidance."

Thus, just as Jesus is presented in the Gospels as having divine authority and being above the Law, so also the community of disciples or church is said to have received from Jesus the authority to define what is acceptable and unacceptable among its members, and to have received the Holy Spirit to assist them in this process. Undoubtedly, they still look to the commandments as an enduring expression of God's will, asking how those commandments apply to their everyday lives; yet because they find themselves in contexts that are in many ways different from the context in which the Law was originally given, they must interpret that Law on the basis of what Jesus taught, and exercise the freedom to bind and loose commandments as he directed them to do.

It is important to note that when Jesus sends his disciples out to proclaim the gospel, he sends them into the places where people lived and worked. They were not to take anything with them, but instead go into people's homes and receive what they were offered, "eating and drinking whatever they provide" (Luke 10:7), just as Jesus himself did. They were not to remain huddled behind closed doors, as they later were doing out of fear on the day of Jesus' resurrection. In this regard, the activity of both Jesus and his disciples stands in contrast to what took place among many teachers and their disciples in antiquity, both in Jewish and pagan circles: in schools where the Torah was studied or where philosophy was taught, discussions were generally held inside of buildings, often behind closed doors where certain people were barred from entering (most notably women and outsiders). This meant that discussions regarding what was right and wrong were carried out in contexts that were *isolated* from the "real world" in which the common people actually lived and moved about. While Jesus no doubt taught his disciples in private at times, it seems that it was more common for him to give instruction regarding God's will for human beings out in the open, where all sorts of people were gathered. Both Jesus and his disciples, then, reached out to others where they were at and considered questions of what was right and wrong in those contexts as they ministered to people's needs and were in dialogue with them, rather than withdrawing into isolation.

The new covenant

Although Jesus sent out disciples to do work during the period of his own ministry, once he had died and risen, the task as well as the message of those sent out changed. Undoubtedly, they believed that in a sense Jesus continued to be with them, as he had promised, and much of their activity of reaching out to others remained the same. In the final hours before his arrest, trial, and crucifixion, however, Jesus had done something of great significance. During his last supper with the disciples, he had taken bread and told them, "This is my body, which is given for you," and then had taken a cup of wine and said, "This cup that is poured out for you is the new covenant in my blood" (Luke 22:19-20).

In the Jewish faith, the concept of covenant was central. Through Moses, God had graciously made a covenant with the descendants of Abraham, Isaac, and Jacob, promising to bless them in many ways. At the same time, however, God had given them the commandments, and told them that they were to obey those commandments in order to remain in the covenant relationship as God's special people. In Exodus 24:3-8, we read of the institution of this covenant. Moses read to the people all of the commandments, and the people promised to do all that the Lord had spoken. Moses then offered up sacrifices to God, and after sprinkling part of the sacrificial blood on the altar, he took the remainder and sprinkled it on the people, referring to it as "the blood of the covenant that the LORD has made with you." From that time on, the covenant had been in force.

The idea of a "new covenant" appears for the first time in Jeremiah 31:31-34, where God promises to "make a new covenant with the house of Israel and the house of Judah." Through Jeremiah, God promised that this covenant would be distinct from the one made previously under Moses, which had been broken: "I will put my law within them, and write it on their hearts; and I will be their God, and they shall be my people. No longer shall they teach one another, or say to each other, 'Know the Lord,' for they shall all know me, from the least of them to the greatest, says the Lord; for I will forgive their iniquity, and remember their sin no more."

When Jesus spoke of a "new covenant," then, he was referring to the establishment of a new relationship between God and those who would belong to this new covenant people.[7] While this covenant also promised forgiveness, life, and other blessings, those promises would no longer be conditioned by the laws given through Moses. From then on, they would be accepted and forgiven by God, not by virtue of their presenting in the Temple the sacrifices prescribed in the Mosaic Law, but by virtue of Jesus' self-offering to God in death on their behalf. Likewise, this new covenant people was called to live in obedience, not simply to the words of the old covenant, but to the words of Jesus. According to John's Gospel, it was at this time that Jesus gave his disciples the "new commandment": "that you love one another, just as I have loved you" (John 13:34, 15:12). As the First Epistle of John explains, however, this "new commandment" is at the same time "an old commandment that you have had from the beginning" (1 John 2:7-8), since in reality, this is what the Mosaic Law already prescribed. While there was, therefore, continuity between the old covenant and the new, so that what was found in the old covenant was not "abolished" but "fulfilled," this new covenant would revolve, not around the Torah, but around Jesus himself, crucified and risen.

Questions for reflection and discussion

1. How do you understand the difference between "following the commandments" and "following Jesus"? What is the relationship between the two ideas?

2. Read one or more of the following passages, noting how Jesus' compassion moved him to action: Matthew 9:35-38, 14:14-21, 20:29-34; Mark 8:1-9; Luke 7:11-16. Do you see the same relation between compassion and action in your own life, in the life of your church and others, and in society today? Where do you see instead attitudes like those of the scribes and Pharisees who opposed Jesus?

3. How did each of the various aspects of Jesus' ministry—teaching, preaching, healing, feeding, accompanying, visiting, praying, preparing disciples, etc.—contribute to making others whole? How do we seek the wholeness of others today through these same activities, both as a church and as individuals, taking Jesus' ministry as our model?

4. In light of their concern for observance of the Law, why do you think the scribes and Pharisees who opposed Jesus got so upset with him for eating and drinking with the "sinners" who did not observe the Law? From your experience, is "shunning" people a good way to get them to change their behavior and their attitudes? Compare that approach with Jesus' approach of accepting sinful people even before they repent, and showing them unconditional love.

4

The Letter and the Spirit in Paul's Thought

By the time Paul began his ministry as an "apostle of Jesus Christ," the situation of Jesus' community of followers had changed a great deal. The most important change was that non-Jews, or Gentiles, had been admitted as members of that community. Their inclusion, however, raised a difficult problem: Was it necessary for them to be circumcised and observe all of the commandments of the Torah, in effect becoming Jews, as Jesus and his first disciples were? According to Acts 15, Paul and the other apostles, together with other members of the church, came together in Jerusalem to decide this question. The decision taken was that the Gentiles might be admitted to the community through Baptism without submitting to circumcision and the Jewish Law; they were merely to abstain from eating certain foods and practicing fornication.

Paul's letters, however, provide evidence that throughout most of his ministry questions related to the observance of the Jewish Law continued to be the cause of conflict and division. Because he carried out his ministry in contexts that were in some ways very different from the contexts in which Jesus had worked in Palestine, Paul also had to deal with new questions and problems that Jesus had never specifically addressed. The way in which he responded to those questions and problems on the basis of both the Jewish Law and Jesus' teaching is of great interest to us today, precisely because we too are faced with decisions regarding questions and problems that are not contemplated in Scripture.

Upholding the Law?

Like Jesus, Paul faced the accusation that he undermined the Law of Moses and taught others to disobey it. This accusation is specifically leveled against him in Acts 21:28, where several Jews from Asia shout excitedly to others gathered in the Temple court, "This is the man who is teaching everyone everywhere against our people, our law, and this place." However, just as Jesus taught that he had not come to abolish the Law but to fulfill it, so Paul insisted that he did not "overthrow" the Law but "upheld" it (Rom. 3:31).

In other passages, however, Paul seems to contradict this claim, since he states that believers are no longer under the Law but are free from it and have died to it (Rom. 6:14-15, 7:4-6; Gal. 2:19, 5:18). To understand Paul's thought, however, we must turn to what he writes in his Epistle to the Romans:

> Circumcision indeed is of value if you obey the law; but if you break the law, your circumcision has become uncircumcision. So, if those who are uncircumcised keep the requirements of the law, will not their uncircumcision be regarded as circumcision? Then those who are physically uncircumcised but keep the law will condemn you that have the written code and circumcision but break the law. For a person is not a Jew who is one outwardly, nor is true circumcision something external and physical. Rather, a person is a Jew who is one inwardly, and real circumcision is a matter of the heart—it is spiritual and not literal (Rom. 2:25-29).

In Jewish thought, it would be a contradiction in terms to say that those who are uncircumcised might "keep the requirements of the law," or to speak of "those who are physically uncircumcised but keep the law." One of the things that the Law commanded was physical circumcision (Gen. 17:12, Lev. 12:3); therefore, a man who had not been circumcised could hardly be said to be observing the Law. We find the same problem in Paul's affirmation in 1 Corinthians

7:19 (RSV): "For neither circumcision counts for anything nor uncircumcision, but keeping the commandments of God." For Jews, to keep the commandments of God meant keeping the commandment regarding circumcision as well.

The key to Paul's thought, however, appears to be in the last phrase from the Romans passage just quoted: "real circumcision is a matter of the heart—it is spiritual and not literal." Literally, these last words say, "circumcision is of the heart, in spirit and not in letter." Here we find the explicit distinction between the spirit and the letter of the Law. This distinction appears twice elsewhere in Paul's epistles. Later, in Romans 7:6, Paul writes that "now we are discharged from the law, dead to that which held us captive, so that we are slaves not under the old written code but in the new life of the Spirit"; the last phrase reads literally, "so that we serve in newness of spirit and not oldness of letter." And in 2 Corinthians 3:6, Paul tells the Corinthians that God "has made us competent to be ministers of a new covenant, not of letter but of spirit; for the letter kills, but the Spirit gives life."

This last phrase sounds strikingly similar to Jesus' question in Mark 3:4 as to whether it is lawful on the sabbath "to save life or to kill." As was the case with Jesus, for Paul true fulfillment of the Law involves observing its spirit. Thus, for example, the circumcision that really counts is not the literal circumcision that Jewish males received when they turned eight days old, but the "circumcision of the heart." In fact, this is the circumcision of which the Law itself speaks. In Deuteronomy Moses tells the people, "Circumcise, then, the foreskin of your heart" (10:16), and then adds further on: "the LORD your God will circumcise your heart and the heart of your descendants, so that you will love the LORD your God with all your heart and with all your soul, in order that you may live" (30:6). In Jeremiah 31 God speaks in similar terms regarding the new covenant: "I will put my law within them, and I will write it on their hearts" (v. 33).

For Paul, then, believers were under a new covenant, and were "dead to" and "discharged from" their previous relation to the old covenant and its law. The continuity between Paul's teaching on the Law and that of Jesus is evident here, as it is in a number of other passages where Paul speaks of fulfilling the Law. In Romans 13:8-10 we read, "the one who loves another has fulfilled the law. The commandments, 'You shall not commit adultery; You shall not murder; You shall not steal; You shall not covet'; and any other commandment, are summed up in this word, 'Love your neighbor as yourself.' Love does no wrong to a neighbor; therefore, love is the fulfilling of the law." A similar statement appears in Galatians 5:14 (RSV): "For the whole law is fulfilled in one word, 'You shall love your neighbor as yourself.'" It can hardly be doubted that Paul is alluding to the teaching of Jesus here, since Jesus also quoted Leviticus 19:18 about loving one's neighbor when asked about what the Law commands.[1] It is important to note Paul's use of the word *fulfill*: what is involved is not the *abolishment* of the law, but its *fulfillment*.

Fulfilling the law of Christ

In a couple of passages Paul refers to the "law of Christ." He writes to the Galatians, "Bear one another's burdens and so fulfill the law of Christ" (Gal. 6:2 RSV). A few years later, he tells the Corinthian community, "To those under the law I became as one under the law (though I myself am not under the law) so that I might win those under the law. To those outside the law I became as one outside the law (though I am not free from God's law but am under Christ's law) so that I might win those outside the law" (1 Cor. 9:20-21).

Scholars have debated whether the "law of Christ" in these passages refers to the Mosaic Law as interpreted by Jesus, or to a separate and new law given by him.[2] In either case, ultimately the allusion must be primarily to the commandment to love others, since this was for Jesus the summary of the Mosaic Law, as well as the new commandment that he gave. For Paul, believers are free from the Mosaic Law in the sense that they are no longer bound to observe its letter, but yet they are "not free from God's law" in the sense that they are still to be obedient to the *spirit* of that law, as taught by Christ.

In the latter of these two passages, Paul indicates that at times he lives "as one under the law," evidently observing the *letter* and not just the *spirit* of the Mosaic commandments. In this regard, it is important to note that, in Jewish thought, the Mosaic Law had not been given to *all* people, but only to God's covenant people Israel. It became common in Judaism to speak of another, universal covenant made by God with all the other nations in Genesis 9:8-17, where God promises Noah that there will be no more floods over all the earth. The covenant made there is said to be between God and "every living creature of all flesh that is on the earth." Later on, it came to be said that this Noahic covenant contained seven commandments for Gentiles, while the covenant made with Israel contained 613, as we noted in chapter 1.

Paul seems to have agreed with the idea that the Mosaic Law had been given only to the Jewish people, and not to all nations. Thus, although believers lived under a new covenant through Christ, those who were of Jewish origin might still live under the letter of the Law, as Paul at times did. In Acts 21, before Paul's arrest, James and the other leaders of the church in Jerusalem tell Paul that a rumor about him is spreading among many of the Jews who are zealous for the Law: "They have been told about you that you teach all the Jews living among the Gentiles to forsake Moses, and that you tell them not to circumcise their children or observe the customs" (v. 21). They then ask Paul to go through a rite of purification with some Jewish believers, so that "all will know that there is nothing in what they have been told about you, but that you yourself observe and guard the law" (v. 24). The fact that Paul accedes to their request demonstrates that, according to Luke, he was not in fact telling Jews not to submit to the Mosaic Law any longer.

The debate in the early church, therefore, was not whether Jewish believers should abandon the Mosaic Law, but whether the Gentile believers had to become Jews first in order to be followers of Jesus. A number of Jewish believers insisted that this was necessary, but Paul and the other apostles rejected that idea. This must be kept in mind when comparing Paul's attitude toward the letter of the Law with that of Jesus. As we noted in chapter 2, at times Jesus is presented as insisting that the letter of the Law must be observed, and not just the spirit. However, Jesus probably agreed with the Judaism of his day in regarding the letter as binding only on Jews, and not on Gentiles. This seems to have been the situation in the early church, although it seems that even Jewish believers like Paul or Peter had the freedom to set aside the letter of the Law when circumstances justified it (see Gal. 2:11-14).

Nevertheless, according to Paul, the Mosaic Law continued to be a guide even for Gentile believers, as is evident in Romans 13:8-10, where he quotes the commandments prohibiting adultery, murder, stealing, and coveting. Paul could hardly have believed that it was no longer necessary to keep these commandments literally, but only to "love one's neighbor"; those commandments are "summed up" in the love commandment, rather than being *replaced* by it. Thus, while what mattered most for Paul was fulfilling the "law of Christ," the letter of the Mosaic Law still had a place in his teaching; he did not simply lay it aside.

Led by the Spirit

For Paul, believers are no longer under the Law of Moses not only because they now live under the law of Christ, but also because they have received the Holy Spirit: "if you are led by the Spirit, you are not subject to the law" (Gal. 5:18). Because they walk according to the Spirit and are guided by that Spirit, the "just requirement of the law" is now fulfilled in them (Rom. 8:4). It should be noted that here, as in Romans 2:26, what is fulfilled is not merely the *Law*, but its "just requirement"; believers practice the justice or righteousness that is the purpose or intent underlying the Law's commandments.

According to Paul, there are two reasons why those who have received the Holy Spirit are no longer subject to the Mosaic Law. First, the Spirit fulfills the function of the Torah in guiding and instructing them, pointing out to them how they are to live. This is essentially the same idea that we noted in the last chapter: because Jesus poured out the Holy Spirit on the disciples, and that Spirit leads and instructs them, they have the authority to make decisions regarding what is acceptable and unacceptable in the life of the community. Through the Spirit, believers receive the "mind of Christ," so that they are able to discern God's will and "judge all things" (1 Cor. 2:10-16). For Paul, the Spirit also enables believers to understand the Law of Moses according to its true meaning or purpose, thus removing the veil that covers the eyes of those who do not know Christ (2 Cor. 3:1-18); this means that they have freedom.

A second reason why those who have the Spirit are no longer subject to the Law is that the Spirit enables them to overcome the power of sin and live according to God's will, albeit imperfectly. The Holy Spirit pours God's love into their hearts (Rom. 5:5), fills them with power (Rom. 15:13), and enables them to overcome the flesh so as to produce fruits that are pleasing to God (Gal. 5:22-23, Rom. 7:4-6). There is a new power in their lives that enables them to live as God's children.

For Paul, all of this involves no longer living in "slavery," but in "freedom." "For freedom Christ has set us free" (Gal. 5:1), in the sense that believers are not under the Mosaic Law, which held people captive in a type of slavery or subjection (Rom. 7:6, Gal. 3:23-25). Nevertheless, they are still "slaves of God" and "slaves of righteousness" or "justice" (Rom. 6:16-22) in the sense that they must keep the

Law's spirit; like the Hebrew word *tsedaqah*, the Greek word *dikaio-sunē*, used here and elsewhere, can rightly be translated "justice" and not merely "righteousness." Believers are "called to freedom" but "through love become slaves to one another" (Gal. 5:13), and serve under the newness of the Spirit (Rom. 7:6). Once again, they are to observe the spirit of the Law and fulfill its "just requirement," yet are not obligated to observe literally all of the precepts of the Torah.

The love commandment in practice

Several passages from Paul's epistles illustrate well his teaching that believers are free from the Law and yet bound to serve others. Questions regarding food were potentially very divisive in the communities to which Paul wrote, since such questions had important implications for table fellowship among those who followed the Jewish customs and kosher laws and those who did not; the matter of whether it was acceptable to eat food that had been sacrificed to idols was also debated.[3] Rather than proposing strict rules about what could or could not be eaten, Paul insists in several passages that all have freedom to do what their conscience dictates, but must not pass judgment on one another (Rom. 14:1-23; 1 Cor. 8:7-13, 10:23-33). The rule Paul does lay down, however, is that no one must do anything that harms the faith or conscience of another; on the contrary, one must behave in a way that seeks the good of others and builds them up: "If your brother or sister is being injured by what you eat, you are no longer walking in love. . . . Everything is indeed clean, but it is wrong for you to make others fall by what you eat" (Rom. 14:15, 20). "We are no worse off if we do not eat, and no better off if we do. But take care that this liberty of yours does not somehow become a stumbling block to the weak" (1 Cor. 8:8-9).

Similarly, when discussing questions of the observance of certain Jewish festivals, which according to the Mosaic Law was obligatory, Paul teaches that believers are free to decide for themselves whether to observe them or not; however, they must not pass judgment on each other and must "be fully convinced in their own minds" (Rom. 14:5, see also Col. 2:16-17). Rather than laying down specific commandments for all to obey, or demanding observance of the Jewish Law, Paul allows for diversity and freedom among believers, as long as all fulfill the Law's spirit and are convinced that they are doing what is right according to their conscience.

Paul applies these same principles to problems unrelated to the Jewish Law that arose in the churches. In Corinth, the fact that some exercised gifts of prophecy and spoke in tongues had created conflict and divisions (1 Corinthians 14). While Paul lays down some guidelines for the Corinthians, even saying that what he writes is "a command of the Lord" (v. 37), he also insists repeatedly that what ultimately matters is love and mutual edification (vv. 1-5, 12, 17-19, 26, 31). It is in this context that he writes what is often called the "love chapter," 1 Corinthians 13. Similarly, when Paul invites the Corinthians to contribute for the collection he is taking up for the "saints" in Jerusalem, he simply exhorts them to be generous, but does not prescribe some specific amount or percentage that they must give, such as a tithe. He gives them "advice" but tells them that as long as one acts out of good will and love for others, whatever one gives is acceptable and constitutes obedience to the gospel of Christ (2 Cor. 8:7-12, 9:7-15). Thus, while Paul himself gave specific instructions to others, he also repeatedly insisted that they had the freedom to do whatever they considered right, as long as they fulfilled the spirit of the Law.

Paul and the teaching of Jesus

If for Paul what really matters is observing the spirit of the Law, what importance does the letter of the Law have? It is important to note that Paul continues to cite commandments from the Law as binding in some sense, as we saw above with regard to several of the Ten Commandments in Romans 13:9; in Ephesians 6:2, the commandment to honor one's father and mother also appears. Elsewhere, however, Paul goes beyond the literal meaning of a commandment: in 1 Corinthians 9:9, discussing the rights of an apostle to receive financial support, he quotes Deuteronomy 25:4, "You shall not muzzle an ox while it is treading out the grain." Paul clarifies that this passage does not refer simply to oxen and derives a deeper principle from it, namely, that those who work in proclaiming the gospel should be able to live from that work. This passage shows that Paul interpreted the Mosaic Law by seeking to derive certain principles from the commandments that might then be applied to concrete questions which the commandment did not originally address.

In discussing questions such as this, Paul also looks to the teaching of Jesus. When Paul writes in 1 Corinthians 9:14, "the Lord commanded that those who proclaim the gospel should get their living by the gospel," he seems to be referring to what Jesus told the seventy as he sent them out: "the laborer deserves to be paid" (Luke 10:7). Similarly, in 1 Corinthians 7:10, he says that the command "that the wife should not separate from her husband" is not his own, but is from the Lord; the allusion appears to be to Jesus' teaching on divorce in Mark 10:11-12.

What is important for us here, however, is that Paul exercises great freedom with regard to what Jesus taught, and even goes beyond it.[4] While offering the Corinthians certain guidelines with regard to marriage in 1 Corinthians 7, for example, he says that they have freedom to do what they consider is best, since all have different gifts and have received something different from the Lord (vv. 7, 17). He also adds his own counsel and opinions to what Jesus commanded, at times even pointing out that what he writes is not a command of Jesus himself (1 Cor. 7:12, 25-26). In fact, immediately after stating that Jesus commanded that a wife should not separate from her husband, he writes: "but if she *does* separate," thus contemplating the possibility that she might do so in spite of Jesus' command (vv. 11-12). In the following verses (vv. 13-15), Paul also adds his own command (not the Lord's) that one should not divorce one's spouse if the spouse consents to live with the believer; yet this means that if the unbelieving spouse does *not* wish to live with the believer, divorce is acceptable, in spite of Jesus' teaching on divorce. Likewise, even though in 1 Corinthians 9 Paul recalls Jesus' command that those proclaiming the gospel should be paid for their ministry, at the same time he writes that he has "not made use of this right" and does not intend to do so (vv. 12, 15). Thus, he does not feel obligated to conform personally to what Jesus commanded.

These passages are significant because they demonstrate that, just as Paul exercised freedom with regard to the commandments of the Mosaic Law, so also he exercised freedom with regard to what Jesus commanded. This means that, for Paul, Jesus' words do not constitute a new "letter of the Law" that simply must be applied in every context; rather, believers have a certain freedom to conform or not conform to Jesus' own instructions, depending on the situation. In Paul's words, "'all things are lawful,' but not all things are beneficial" or "build up" (1 Cor. 10:23); for him, this is what ultimately mattered.

Questions for reflection and discussion

1. Compare Paul's affirmation that "the letter kills, but the spirit gives life" (2 Cor. 3:6) with Jesus' question as to whether it is lawful "to do good or to do harm on the sabbath, to save life or to kill" (Mark 3:4).

2. In your everyday life, and in the Christian life in general, how do you understand and apply Paul's teaching that we are "free from the law," and yet must still live as "slaves of justice" or righteousness, fulfilling the "just requirement" of the Law?

3. Read Galatians 2:11-14 (noting that "Cephas" is Aramaic for "Peter"). In the eyes of Paul, what did Peter do wrong? When was

he observing the letter of the Law but violating its spirit? When was he observing the spirit but violating the letter? How is this passage relevant for us today?

4. Read Romans 14, and then reflect on how Paul's teaching can be applied to different issues we face today.

5

Looking to the Letter and the Spirit

Reading Scripture is no easy task. Often it is difficult enough simply to make sense of what we read. When we attempt to define questions of right and wrong or seek moral guidance from Scripture, however, the task of interpretation becomes even more difficult. It may seem easy simply to apply directly to our everyday life certain passages where we find clear commands about what to do and not to do. Yet for reasons we have seen in the previous chapters, and which we will consider further here, such a way of reading Scripture can in fact lead to interpretations that run contrary to the spirit of Scripture, and that therefore represent misreadings of Scripture. In order to read and interpret Scripture properly, we need to follow the guidelines and principles that Scripture itself lays out for us, so as to let "Scripture interpret Scripture."

How Scripture is *not* to be interpreted

Perhaps the most important principle of interpretation, as well as the most surprising one for many, is the principle just mentioned: that, *if we are to be faithful to Scripture, we cannot simply apply commandments and precepts from Scripture directly to our present-day contexts*. For example, we cannot simply conclude on the basis of certain passages from Scripture that God prohibits divorce, or homosexuality, or women serving in pastoral roles. Astonishing as it may sound, the same is even true of other commandments, such as those that prohibit killing, adultery, stealing, and bearing false witness, or even the commandment to love one's neighbor! Yet before anyone jumps to the conclusion that we can now throw out the Ten Commandments, it is necessary to understand what is involved.

The reason why commandments from Scripture cannot be applied directly to our present-day contexts is that those commandments, like Scripture in general, were addressed to people who lived in places and times very different from our own, and thus require interpretation. In fact, very few people in our context can even read what was actually written, simply because it was written in other languages. We need someone to translate Scripture for us, and any translation is itself an interpretation. For example, should the Fifth Commandment be translated, "You shall not kill," or "You shall not murder"? In either case, precisely what is prohibited?

Some might claim that what is forbidden in this commandment is quite clear and obvious, and thus that there really is no difficulty of interpretation. Jesus, however, interpreted this commandment as prohibiting becoming angry with one's brother or sister, insulting him or her, or calling him or her a fool (Matt. 5:21-23). Because this interpretation comes from Jesus' lips, as Christians we would no doubt consider it a valid one, although it is certainly not the most obvious interpretation, and probably not the way the commandment was originally intended. Yet even Jesus' own words need further interpretation, given the fact that Jesus himself got angry (Mark 3:5) and called the scribes and Pharisees "fools" (Matt. 23:17).

The fact that we cannot simply apply all of the biblical commandments directly to our present-day contexts becomes obvious when we consider that certain biblical commandments are clearly outdated. Some commandments are even impossible to observe today, such as those having to do with sacrificial worship at the sanctuary designated by God. Other commandments, however, while not impossible to observe, are simply not acceptable in our present-day contexts. Virtually no one today advocates stoning to death those who have committed adultery or children who have cursed their parents, in spite of God's commandment to do so in Leviticus 20:9-10. Nor is it permissible to buy people as slaves and own them as property, as Leviticus 25:44-46 prescribes. We no longer consider it problematic to plant two different kinds of seeds in a field or wear a garment made from two different materials (Lev. 19:19); even the Jubilee laws commanding that fields be left fallow and debts be cancelled every seventh year are scarcely observable in today's world (Lev. 25:1-24, Deut. 15:1).

In response to this problem, it has often been the custom among Christians to make distinctions among the commandments. It is said that there are different types of laws in the Old Testament: the cultic or ceremonial law, the civil law, and the moral law, so as then to argue that Christians are obligated to keep only the moral law, particularly the Ten Commandments. No such distinction is found either in the Bible itself or in ancient Judaism, however; in fact, commandments of different types appear alongside each other as part of a single law (see, for example, Lev. 19:1-12). *All* of the Law was regarded as God's inspired word. To maintain that the ceremonial and civil laws are no longer applicable would also involve throwing out a good part of the Old Testament, as if we might now take a marker to our Bible and cross out the majority of commandments from the Mosaic Law since they no longer apply! Jesus claimed to have come not to *abolish* the Law, but to *fulfill* it.

Jesus as our eternal "Torah"

As Christians, our understanding of Scripture is different from that which has existed in some Jewish circles, where the Torah has been seen as eternal and universal. To maintain that the Torah existed before creation, and that the world was made for the Torah, is to affirm that its commandments are *not* contextual, bound to a particular time and place, but apply to all times and places. As Christians, we instead see the Mosaic Law as something given to a particular people, Israel, in a particular historical context, with the purpose of promoting justice and *shalom* in that time and place. In our own time and place, we would consider many of those commandments cruel and even barbaric rather than just, such as those that prescribe stoning people to death or that allow for the purchase of slaves.

According to the New Testament, it is not the Torah nor the Bible itself that is eternal, but God's Son, Jesus Christ our Lord: "In the beginning was the Word, and the Word was with God, and the Word was God. He was in the beginning with God. All things came into being through him" (John 1:1-3). "All things have been created through him and for him" (Col. 1:16). We might say that, for us as Christians, Jesus is our "Torah," our "guide" and "instruction," like the Holy Spirit. Jesus is the Alpha and the Omega, the criterion for judging all things.

This means that we are to interpret Scripture from the perspective of Jesus, with the "mind of Christ" (1 Cor. 2:16, Phil. 2:4-5). We apply the same principles he did, looking to the *spirit* of God's Law to interpret that Law. As people sent out by Jesus, we follow him in reaching out to others so as to serve as God's instruments for making them whole, as we ourselves are made whole. We are defined, not by the Law alone, but by Jesus, who is greater than the Law. And because Jesus' ministry was a ministry of *justice*—understanding justice as *shalom* for *all*—we too seek justice for all people (including ourselves). This is God's will, and the goal and purpose of God's Law; therefore, any interpretation of the Law that is not faithful to the spirit of the Law cannot rightly be regarded as an expression of God's will, or be said to be in continuity with Jesus' teaching.

Freedom and the Spirit

As Christians, we must take seriously Paul's teaching regarding the freedom that Christians have from the letter of the Law, which Paul ultimately derived from the teaching and example of Jesus himself. "We are discharged from the law," so as to "serve in the newness of the spirit and not the oldness of the letter" (Rom. 7:6*). "If you are led by the Spirit, you are not subject to the law" (Gal. 5:18). "We are not under law but under grace" (Rom. 6:15).

As we saw in the previous two chapters, Jesus gave his disciples (and thus the church) the authority to "bind and loose," that is, to define what is acceptable and not acceptable in the community on the basis of the Law, and also poured out the Holy Spirit on them to guide them in this process. As Paul states, Christians are not under the Law precisely because they have God's Spirit. Of course, as they seek to discern God's will under the Spirit's guidance, they look to the Scriptures, including both the Old and the New Testaments. While as Christians we believe that we are no longer under the old covenant, or Old Testament, since we now live under the new covenant established by Christ, nevertheless we continue to look to the Old Testament for guidance as well, since the new covenant is based upon the old and is in continuity with it, *fulfilling* it rather than *replacing* it.

One of the basic beliefs held by Christians is that the Holy Scriptures were inspired by the Holy Spirit of God, and for that reason possess divine authority. While it is important to stress this doctrine, it is also important that it be understood correctly. We believe that the Holy Spirit inspired the biblical authors to write what they wrote *to a specific audience in a particular time and place*. In the New Testament, for example, we find epistles from Paul addressed to the Romans, to the Corinthians, to the Galatians, to Philemon, and to a number of other churches and individuals. We do not have, however, any epistles addressed by Paul "to all Christians everywhere of all generations until the world comes to an end." Paul's writings, like all the other biblical writings, are *contextual*, written for particular contexts, and we believe that as he wrote to those contexts Paul was inspired by the Holy Spirit.

We also believe, of course, that the Holy Spirit was active to preserve all the writings we find in our Scriptures, and guided the church so that these writings might be gathered and selected to form a canon, that is, a collection of authoritative writings for the church. Yet while it is important to recall what the Holy Spirit did in the *past,* we must also remember what the Spirit does in the *present.* As we read these writings that God's Spirit inspired, preserved, and gathered, that same Spirit *continues to speak to us and guide us* so that we may interpret them properly and apply them to our present-day contexts. If we focus only on what the Spirit communicated *in the past* through the *letter* of the Scriptures, but forget that the Spirit *continues to speak in the present* through those Scriptures, constantly communicating new things to us, we end up misinterpreting the Scriptures, and disregard their *spirit.* Because of the ongoing activity of the Spirit among us, the Scriptures *guide* us, but they do not *bind* us.

This means that as Christians who continue to be led by the Holy Spirit today, we have freedom with regard to the letter found in those Scriptures. Yet while we are free in that respect, we continue to be "servants" or "slaves" in another respect, as Paul teaches: we are slaves of righteousness, or justice (Rom. 6:18). God's will is that we still observe the spirit of the Law, practicing the justice it demands, fulfilling the "just requirement of the law" (Rom. 8:4).

It is also important to remember that this freedom, together with the authority to "bind and loose," is given to Christians *together* as the body of Christ, just as the Scriptures and the Holy Spirit have been given to the church collectively. Therefore, we are called to interpret Scripture and define God's will *in dialogue with one another.* We see this process, for example, in Acts 15, where the first believers came together to decide the question of whether Gentiles needed to be circumcised and observe the Law of Moses, a question that Jesus had never addressed. Those gathered listened to each other carefully, consulted the Scriptures ("the words of the prophets," 15:15), and then came to a decision *together,* claiming that this decision was what "seemed good to the Holy Spirit" (15:28). The Holy Spirit speaks, not only through the Scriptures, but through people as well, and thus we must seek to discern the Spirit's voice in the voices of our sisters and brothers through dialogue.

No spirit without the letter

If Christians are free from the letter of the Law due to their being guided by the spirit (and the Spirit), of what importance is the letter? If the letter of the Law is not abolished, yet Christians are not subject to it, what role does it continue to play? To answer these questions, it is important to underscore once more that, although the letter is bound to specific contexts, it is nevertheless inspired by God's Spirit, who spoke through the biblical authors to God's people in a particular time and place. The letter of the Law, therefore, is of great importance, since as we understand what the Spirit had to say in the contexts in which Scripture was written, we are able to understand what the Spirit has to say today in our own contexts. In other words, *we cannot understand the spirit of the Law without the letter of the Law*, since the two are indissolubly united; in fact, the spirit cannot exist without the letter.

When we speak of things such as justice, wholeness, and well-being, we must remember that these are abstract concepts until they exist in concrete situations. Because of this, if we are to seek these things in accordance with the spirit of God's law, that law must prescribe concrete actions. For example, in Old Testament times, the spirit of the Law took shape through commandments such as the ones prescribing rest once a week, provisions for the poor and weak of society, the cancellation of debts every seven years, and the protection of aliens residing in the land of Israel. Thus, as we read and study laws such as these in their original contexts, we gain a clearer understanding of the ways in which the spirit of the Law can be applied in our contexts today through specific laws, guidelines, and rules.

The commandment to love our neighbor provides us with another example of this. In order to understand what is being commanded of us when we are told to love our neighbor, we must define precisely what Scripture means by love. To do this, we must see what that love looks like in particular contexts, since it can be understood in ways that are unfaithful to what was intended when God gave that commandment. People often justify things such as adultery, stealing, or even violence toward others in the name of love, in reality doing harm to others and to themselves in spite of their claim that they are only seeking what is best for all. Similar problems can arise when love is understood primarily in terms of "good intentions"; throughout history, a tremendous amount of suffering and harm has been occasioned by sincere, caring people whose actions were carried out with the best of intentions, yet who did not listen to or understand those whom they were attempting to help or serve. In this regard, it is important to observe that when Jesus tells his disciples, "Love one another," he immediately adds, *as I have loved you*" (John 13:34). We can only understand the kind of love Jesus was speaking about when we see that love in action in specific contexts, such as his own life and death.

Of course, in order to understand the original contexts in which Scripture was written, we need the work of scholars, that is, the equivalent of what the scribes and Pharisees and teachers of the Law were in biblical times (though, of course, we need the good kind, and not the kind that Jesus described as hypocrites and whitewashed sepulchres!). Paul's epistles also mention "teachers" as essential components of Christ's body the church (1 Cor. 12:28-29, Eph. 4:11). Just as the vast majority of Christians need skilled scholars and teachers to translate Scripture into their own language if they are to understand it, so they also need scholars and teachers to explain to them the original contexts of Scripture and to guide them in their reading of Scripture, as Philip did for the Ethiopian eunuch who was unable to understand Scripture on his own (Acts 8:26-39).

In order to understand the spirit of the Law, therefore, we need to understand the letter in its own context. Then, on that basis, we can consider concrete ways in which we may seek to ensure that the spirit of the Law is fulfilled in our contexts today. Divorced from the letter, the spirit becomes some vague, abstract concept that is devoid of any real meaning, and therefore is easily subject to manipulation and misuse.

No letter without the spirit

Just as we need the letter of the Law in order to understand the spirit of Scripture, so also we need the spirit of the Law in order to understand the letter of Scripture. As was stressed above, *any interpretation of the letter of Scripture that is not faithful to the spirit of the Law is a misinterpretation of Scripture.* This was the error of which Jesus accused his opponents: by neglecting the spirit of the Law and merely focusing on its letter, they fell into interpretations of Scripture that were oppressive, unjust, and unmerciful.

In order to be faithful to the spirit of the Law today, in some cases we may reject or dismiss certain commandments of Scripture, such as those already mentioned having to do with stoning people to death or purchasing slaves. In many cases, however, we will adopt wholeheartedly and unreservedly commandments found in Scripture, such as the commandments not to kill or murder and not to commit adultery. The reason we continue to accept commandments such as these is not because they are included in the Ten Commandments, as if these were still binding due to their forming part of the moral law, in contrast to the ceremonial and civil laws that are no longer applicable. After all, the commandment to refrain from all forms of work every seventh day is also one of the Ten Commandments, as is the Commandment not to make images, which Lutherans usually include under the First Commandment; yet most Christians have traditionally not observed either of these commandments literally. Rather, we accept the commandments prohibiting murder and adultery because the *spirit* of God's Law demands that we do so;

such things are *by their very nature* incompatible with human well-being and wholeness, since they involve doing harm to people and relationships.

Of course, we must still interpret these commandments, defining precisely what constitutes adultery, or what type of killing this commandment prohibits. To do this, we take into account the spirit of the Law once more, in dialogue with one another and seeking direction from God's Spirit. We are concerned both with the literal application of commandments such as these in our everyday life, but also with the deeper meaning of these commandments, as we find in the teaching of Jesus. Thus, we understand adultery to be prohibited both in a literal sense, but also in the sense described by Jesus when he said that whoever looks at another with lust is guilty of adultery (Matt. 5:28). The same is true with the commandment not to kill, which is to be understood both literally and in the deeper sense mentioned by Jesus when he says not to get angry with one's brother or sister, or call him or her a fool.

Even when we look at the deeper, spiritual sense of these commandments, however, they still require interpretation. When Jesus got angry with some of the scribes and Pharisees and called them "fools," he did so out of a concern for justice and human wholeness. He was upset that they wanted to prevent him from helping a person in need (Mark 3:5), and justified injustice and oppression in the name of God's law (Matthew 23). Thus his concern was for the well-being of others, but also for the well-being of those scribes and Pharisees themselves; he addressed them in such harsh terms because he wanted them to change their ways, not only for the good of others, but for their own good.

Just as we cannot apply Jesus' command not to get angry to every situation—and in fact sometimes must do exactly the opposite of what his words prescribe by becoming angry as he did in the face of injustice—so also we must similarly interpret everything else Jesus says in the Gospels. In other words, not only do we interpret the commandments of the Old Testament in the way taught by Jesus, examining their spirit together with their letter, but we also interpret the teaching of Jesus himself in the same way. That is, we do not apply Jesus' words literally and directly to every context, but seek to discern the spirit underlying them so as to be faithful to that spirit.

As we saw in the last chapter, this is how Paul interpreted Jesus' teaching. Rather than applying everything Jesus taught literally and directly to the new contexts he faced, he sought to be faithful to the spirit of Jesus' teaching in addressing problems and questions such as those that existed in the church in Corinth. And just as Paul was being faithful to Jesus' teaching by not simply applying Jesus' own words literally and directly to his own context, in order for us to be faithful to the teaching of both Jesus and Paul, we must also avoid applying their words literally and directly to our contexts today without first considering the spirit behind those words. Paul's command in Romans 13:1-7 to be subject to the governing authorities, for example, cannot simply be applied literally to every situation as a universal law, but must be interpreted on the basis of the spirit of God's law, taking into account both the original context in which Paul wrote those words as well as our contexts today. At times, simply to submit to the authorities may be contrary to God's will, as is evident when we consider contexts where oppressive regimes or leaders commit grave injustices and even atrocities.

No doubt, this may sound contradictory: to be faithful to what the Bible, Jesus, and Paul teach, we must *not* apply their teaching directly, but instead must interpret it and in some cases go against its letter so as to keep its spirit. Of course, in some cases, we will end up keeping the letter virtually intact, as is the case with the commandments regarding murder and adultery. But ultimately, our concern is with the spirit; while we need the letter of God's law, that letter must always be interpreted in the light of the spirit of God's law.

Questions for reflection and discussion

1. On the basis of Scripture, how would you respond to those Christians who apply commandments and passages from the Bible directly to our present-day contexts in order to define right and wrong, without taking into account the spirit of God's law?

2. Reflect on the fact that Jesus prohibited getting angry or calling one's brother or sister a "fool," yet did the same things himself in certain circumstances. What does this tell us about the way we are to interpret and apply biblical commandments?

3. How do we understand the Holy Spirit's *past* work of inspiring the Scriptures in relation to the Spirit's *present, ongoing* work in enabling us to understand, interpret, and apply those Scriptures? What problems arise if we neglect the latter aspect of the Spirit's work?

4. Explain in your own words the principles of "no spirit without the letter" and "no letter without the spirit."

6

Discerning God's Will Today

The world in which we live is a complex one, much more so than the world of biblical times. We face problems and issues of which the writers of Scripture never dreamed. Even many of the age-old problems and issues that they did address, such as those having to do with social and economic justice, interpersonal relationships, and health concerns, have grown in complexity since their time.

In spite of the enormous distance in time that separates us from the writers of Scripture, as Christians we believe that what they wrote is still timely and relevant for us today, and thus look to those writings to discern what we believe to be God's will for our lives and our world. As we do so, of course, we must follow the principles and guidelines laid out in Scripture that have been the subject of our study so far. In this final chapter, we will look at ways in which those principles and guidelines can be applied to a number of the concrete issues and questions we face today in a way that is faithful to Scripture. A good place to begin is with several of the issues raised in this book's introduction.

The question of divorce

We have already examined briefly Jesus' teaching on divorce in chapter 2. It should be clear that the context in which Jesus spoke is in some ways quite different from that in which we live today. In our society, divorce is not about a man simply sending his wife away for whatever reason, perhaps in an oppressive and unjust manner; in fact, our laws no longer permit a man to send his wife away in the way the Mosaic Law allowed. There are laws protecting both spouses, and ensuring that each is provided for, together with any children they may have. Furthermore, divorce is essentially an official recognition that a marital relationship has reached a point in which it can no longer continue; in that sense, divorce does not so much put an end to the relationship as it does recognize that the relationship has already ended.

Of course, as Jesus' words indicate, divorce is not a good thing and does not represent God's original will for human beings. It is extremely painful for all involved. Yet when a marital relationship reaches a point where it is more harmful to continue the marriage than to end it, not only for one or both of the spouses but for the children as well, then we may consider divorce to be justified and acceptable as the lesser of two evils. The basis for such a consideration is precisely our concern for *human wholeness and well-being:* in this case, to prohibit divorce would do more harm than good. In addition, our concern for the well-being of persons who have been divorced may lead us to rejoice with them when they find someone else with whom they wish to share their lives in a marital relationship, and thus to bless that new relationship in a marriage ceremony at church. In these situations, we remember that it is "not good" for a man or a woman to be alone, according to God's original intention in creation (see Gen. 2:18).

Of course, it is important to look to the letter of Jesus' teaching and not just its spirit. On the basis of that teaching, we must do everything possible to strengthen and save marriages, and must not take divorce and remarriage lightly. Jesus expresses an ideal in his teaching on divorce, and we strive to attain that ideal. Similarly, before we bless a new marriage, we generally insist that the couple receive adequate counseling so that mistakes made in the past are not repeated. Yet in order to be faithful to Jesus' teaching as a whole, we must apply the principles of interpretation given by Jesus himself to what he says regarding divorce. To adhere strictly to the *letter* of what Jesus taught in his own particular historical context by refusing to accept divorce and remarriage today under any circumstances would involve violating the *spirit* of his teaching. While Jesus' concern for human well-being and justice led him to teach as he did on divorce in his own context, the fact that much has changed since then means that it is not acceptable to apply his teaching literally and directly to our contexts today.

The position of women in home and church

How do we deal with the teaching we find in the Pauline epistles regarding the subjection of women to men? When we look at those passages in their original contexts, it appears that the concern behind them was that of maintaining order in home and community. For example, in the passages from Ephesians 5:22-33 and Colossians 3:18, where wives are told to be subject to their husbands, the concern seems to be for preserving the traditional social structures to avoid conflict in the home and the church, and to avoid provoking the hostility of outsiders.[1] The same concerns appear to be behind the passages that prescribe that women should keep silent and not exercise authority over men (1 Cor. 14:34-35, 1 Tim. 2:11-12). The fact that elsewhere in the New Testament we read of women teaching men, speaking publicly in the church, and exercising leadership roles makes it clear that the Pauline passages just mentioned were directed to very specific contexts and situations, and did not even apply everywhere during Paul's day (see Acts 18:24-26; Rom. 16:1; 1 Cor. 11:5, 13).

Of course, at times theological and biblical arguments are presented so as to provide a foundation for these prescriptions; it is said that women should not exercise authority over men because God is the head of Christ (1 Cor. 11:3), or because Eve was created after Adam from his rib and it was she who was deceived by the serpent (1 Tim. 2:11-14). Yet even these arguments are contextual, in that they begin by assuming a certain position and then seek to find a biblical basis for it. One could just as easily develop contrary arguments from Scripture, claiming, for example, that since women beget men by giving birth to them, men should be subject to women as Christ is subject to God, since God begat Christ (see 1 Cor. 11:12). Similarly, one might argue that because Adam failed to fulfill his responsibility to watch over Eve and exercise authority over her, and did not repudiate her action but did the same, he has forfeited that authority. Thus, theological and biblical arguments can be developed in support of opposing positions.

In any case, the position of women in our society today is quite different from their position in the society of Paul's day. The claim that order in the home, in church, and in society can only be maintained by subjecting women to men is simply no longer tenable. While in earlier times many in the church were convinced that, for the church's own welfare and for it to accomplish its mission effectively in certain contexts, it was often necessary for women to be subject to men and not exercise leadership roles, today churches such as the Evangelical Lutheran Church in America have concluded the opposite: the church cannot be whole and carry out its mission effectively without ordaining women into the pastoral ministry and working to ensure full equality between women and men. When women are excluded from leadership roles, not only do they suffer, but the church and those it serves suffer as well. Thus, by including women in those roles, the church is being faithful to the spirit of Paul's teaching as a whole, showing concern for what edifies, rather than rejecting his teaching. It is also exercising the freedom and authority given to it by Christ to make such decisions, convinced that as it does so, it is being guided by the Holy Spirit, who speaks to the church ever anew.

The issue of homosexuality

A much more controversial subject is that of homosexuality. Up until recent times, it was customary for most Christians simply to condemn homosexual relationships on the basis of biblical passages such as Leviticus 18:22 and 20:13, Romans 1:26-32, 1 Corinthians 6:9-10, and 1 Timothy 1:9-11. Once more, however, it must be stressed that we cannot simply apply such passages directly to our present-day contexts. A number of studies have argued that what was being condemned was something quite different from the type of relationship that exists among many homosexual couples today, in which both partners are committed to love and be faithful to one another throughout life.[2]

Whatever position one takes with regard to homosexuality in the church, what is important is that, in order to be faithful to Scripture, the discussion must focus on the question of what contributes to human wholeness and well-being in our day and age. Those in favor of blessing committed relationships between persons of the same sex and allowing persons living in such relationships to serve in the public ministry of the church argue that these things are necessary, not only for homosexual persons themselves to experience wholeness and well-being in their lives, but for the church to be healthy and whole. This can only happen if the church is fully inclusive of all people who wish to belong to it, regardless of their sexual orientation. From this perspective, to do otherwise is to sin against Christ and to go *against* what he and the Scriptures teach us. The church cannot advocate for justice when it practices injustice and oppression in its own midst.

Those who oppose the blessing of same-sex relationships and the acceptance of gay and lesbian persons into the church's public ministry would argue that homosexual relationships are harmful not only for the individuals who are homosexual but also for church and society as a whole. According to what we have seen previously, in order to apply the Scripture passages just mentioned to our present-day contexts, one would first need to deal with the question of *why* those passages condemn sexual relations between people of the same gender, since the *letter* of God's law can only be regarded as binding today when it is shown that it still reflects faithfully the *spirit* of that law.

One would also need to respond to the argument that the behavior being condemned in the contexts in which Scripture was written is something different than what is being advocated as acceptable today.

If the discussion of this subject can revolve around the question of human wholeness and well-being, so that all those involved in the discussion are speaking out of love and concern for others, perhaps that discussion might be less heated than it has often been in the past. The manner in which Jesus carried out his ministry, giving priority to *people* rather than *laws* and reaching out in dialogue to others with a spirit of acceptance rather than condemnation, must also be taken into account. To be faithful to Jesus, we must enter into dialogue with one another and seek to understand things from the perspective of others, rather than simply cite biblical commandments so as to condemn people without listening to them, as the scribes and Pharisees who opposed Jesus tended to do.

It may also be helpful here to consider what we saw in chapter 4 concerning Paul's teaching about food questions in Romans 14 and 1 Corinthians 8 and 10. While these questions might seem to be of minimal importance for us today, the subject was a very divisive one in the early Christian communities, as these passages and others (such as Gal. 2:11-14) demonstrate; many no doubt felt as strongly about food questions as some Christians feel today about the question of homosexuality. In these passages, Paul allows for different practices, only insisting that Christians not judge one another, not harm the faith of one another, or go against what their conscience tells them to be right and acceptable before God. To be faithful to Scripture, at times we need to follow this same approach to many of the questions that divide us; perhaps the question of homosexuality is one issue demanding such an approach.

Other contemporary ethical questions

Many of the ethical questions we face today are profoundly complex, making it impossible to do justice to them here. This is true with respect to the question of abortion, which was raised in the introduction, as well as many other questions, such as euthanasia, physician-assisted suicide, genetic engineering, human cloning, surrogacy, ecological and environmental concerns, and capital punishment. Ethical decisions are also required with respect to other social and political issues, including war, immigration, public social programs, and fair trade.

Most of these issues are not dealt with explicitly in Scripture. Even when Scripture does seem to speak to some of them indirectly, such as when it prohibits killing, interpretation is required. Killing may be justified in some circumstances, such as a just war. Some people argue that taking life is also justified when the pain experienced by those with a terminal illness is too great for them to bear. Because it is not clear at what point a fetus can be considered a human person, the commandment not to kill may not always apply to abortion. Even those who believe it does may admit that under certain circumstances abortion is permissible, such as when a woman's life is in danger or a pregnancy is the result of rape or incest.

If Scripture does not speak directly to many of these issues, then how can we use it to address them? Clearly, in light of what has been argued so far, we need to focus on the spirit of God's law, raising questions having to do with human well-being, *shalom,* and justice. This is not a simple task. It is necessary to ask, not only about what is best for particular individuals, but for families and other human communities, as well as society in general. This is true not only with regard to physical or material concerns, but spiritual, emotional, psychological, and social concerns as well. Future generations must also be taken into account, as is particularly evident with regard to the ecological and environmental challenges we face today.

In discussing these questions, those who are particularly affected by them must be heard. One can hardly address a subject such as abortion, for example, without seeking to understand the reality of women who choose to terminate an unwanted pregnancy, particularly those living in conditions of great hardship. We must approach those who face difficult decisions with the same spirit shown by Jesus, a spirit of gracious acceptance and compassion, helping them to reflect on the issues by examining a variety of perspectives and alternatives, and supporting them with a nonjudgmental attitude. Naturally, this involves looking at Scripture, praying, and trusting that God's Spirit will provide the necessary guidance. What must be avoided is defining unilaterally what is best for others, claiming the right to determine God's will for others on the basis of one's own interpretation of Scripture, without examining other interpretations or listening to the ways in which God's Spirit speaks to others. This type of approach is precisely what Jesus found so offensive in many of the scribes and Pharisees.

Most of the difficult ethical questions we face today in society are already being addressed by Christians who have studied these questions in great detail and with much serious reflection.[3] It is important that we listen carefully to all the different voices in these discussions, placing ourselves together with others under the gospel of Christ so as to define God's will jointly through dialogue. The Spirit may lead us to reach a consensus, as occurred in Acts 15 when the question of whether Gentile believers had to observe the Law was discussed; or the Spirit may instead lead us to take different views on certain matters, and to respect one another's conscience on those matters, as Paul taught. Either way, we must seek God's will in dialogue with one another, so as to "pursue what makes for peace and for mutual upbuilding" (Rom. 14:19). At the center of our discussion must be the concern we all share for the wholeness and well-being of all. This means that, in spite of our differences on these questions, we remain *united to one another in a spirit of love, caring, and compassion,* rather than seeing those whose ideas differ from ours as our enemies or as enemies of God.

Questions raised by Scripture

Not only do we look to Scripture for answers to questions that arise in our present-day contexts; we must also look to Scripture to see what questions it raises for *us* to answer. For example, what concerns does the commandment to rest on the sabbath raise for us today? The vast majority of Christians no longer observe this commandment literally as the Jewish people have traditionally done. Yet once we have grasped the intent behind it—namely, the need for periodic rest so that we may enjoy life and good health—we must ask whether we are fulfilling its spirit today. While this involves examining our own lives, both as individuals and as families, it also involves looking at the laws in our society to see whether this need is being fulfilled properly. The fact that the Old Testament prescribes that the resident alien and animals were also to rest on the sabbath, and that even the land was to have a sabbath rest, means that we must also be concerned about other people and other living things, as well as God's creation in general. The lack of such rest is an increasing problem today in our "24/7" society and in our world where people and resources, especially in poorer countries, are mercilessly exploited for the benefit of a few, such as those living in wealthy nations.[4]

Commandments like those prescribing that the edges of the fields be left unharvested and that debts be canceled every seven years also present challenges to us. In our contexts today, of course, the best way to take care of the poor is not simply to leave some of the crops unharvested. We must seek other ways of more equal distribution of food. Just as God continually insisted in Old Testament times that both the land and what it produced belonged to God and thus were to be used as God commanded, so also today we must recover the notion that the earth and its resources belong to God and are given to all of us in order that we may care for one another with justice. This may require that we question the increasing privatization of resources and develop a greater sense of responsibility for the welfare of those in greatest need.

The biblical commandments, therefore, can illuminate our examination of social justice issues today. In a nation of immigrants such as the United States, for example, the biblical laws prescribing care for migrants and foreigners and the protection of their basic human rights must be looked to for guidance. The issue of individuals, communities, and entire nations being driven deeply into debt in order to survive is as much a problem today as it was in biblical times. While it is probably not feasible to cancel debts entirely every seven years, we must seek other ways to deal with this problem, as well as similar problems. The recent international Jubilee campaigns for debt alleviation for poorer countries have looked to the Jubilee laws found in the Old Testament for inspiration and guidance.[5] In the United States today, 1 percent of the population owns as much as the lower 90 percent combined, and similar proportions are found in other countries throughout the world. Many of the Old Testament laws were designed to prevent such unequal distribution of wealth, and as we study them and are inspired by them, we can find ways to promote greater justice and equity in the world. This involves going beyond what those laws literally prescribed in their original contexts in order to discover how the principles behind them can be applied today.

Discerning God's will in our personal lives

Just as we look to Scripture for guidance in resolving larger social questions, we also seek guidance there for decisions we must make in our everyday personal lives. In doing so, we apply the same basic principles of interpretation, looking both at the letter and the spirit, but at the same time recognizing our freedom in relation to the letter in order to fulfill the spirit. Here again, discerning God's will for our lives involves not only looking to Scripture for answers to the questions that arise in our lives, but letting Scripture raise questions for us to answer, in order to examine whether we are living in a way that is faithful to the gospel and fulfilling God's law by actively seeking wholeness and justice for all, as Scripture commands.

Interpreting God's will for our lives, of course, is a complex task. For example, we are commanded to love others and seek their well-being, yet also to love ourselves and seek our own well-being: "love your neighbor *as yourself*" (Matt. 22:39). Often the Christian ideal is expressed in terms of "denying oneself" so as to dedicate oneself entirely to serving others. While Jesus certainly commands this in passages such as Luke 9:23, even in the case of this command we must seek to understand and fulfill the spirit of what Jesus is saying. In fact, we can only love others if we love ourselves as God loves us. If we do not take care of our own needs, we cannot care for the needs of others. What is required is that we establish a proper balance between seeking our own well-being and that of others. Even seeking the well-being of others requires balancing our commitment to the well-being of those closest to us, such as our family members, with our commitment to seeking the well-being of people outside of our immediate circle who suffer needs, both in our own communities and societies and in other places around the world.

Applying God's law properly also requires that we discern when to adhere strictly to that law and when to be flexible. In some cases, justice requires "zero tolerance," such as in the case of sexual abuse or drug abuse. In other cases, however, justice requires that we be flexible and forgiving when a strict application of some rule or law would be unjust and oppressive, doing greater harm than good.

Firm in freedom

As we seek to do God's will in our world, as Christians we must "stand firm" in the freedom for which Christ has set us free (Gal. 5:1). For many Christians, the claim that we are free with regard to the letter of the Law in order to fulfill its spirit is a dangerous one. Like many of the Pharisees, they insist that to practice such freedom runs contrary to God's will and leads to moral relativism, where "anything goes," and ultimately all sorts of behavior can be justified by appealing to the spirit of God's law. Instead, they would argue that interpreting Scripture involves a simple, clear-cut, and straight-forward process, in which we apply literally what we read in Scripture to our present-day reality: "This is what the Bible says, in black and white. Period. End of discussion."

While it is important to stress once more that we must not separate the spirit of God's law from its letter, we must always remember that if we are to be faithful to Jesus and the gospel he proclaimed, our primary concern must be with the spirit. The ultimate concern of the authors of the Old Testament, as well as Jesus and Paul, was not to lay down universal, inflexible commandments to which people should blindly submit, but to bring wholeness, justice, peace, and well-being into the lives of human beings. This can only be accomplished when we hold firm to our freedom in Christ, while at the same time submitting as "servants" or "slaves," not to the letter of Scripture, but to justice, as Paul teaches. To live in such freedom undoubtedly is a difficult and risky enterprise, often full of ambiguities and uncertainty; but if we are truly to do God's will, we can live in no other way.

Questions for reflection and discussion

1. Compare what women were doing in 1 Corinthians 11:5, 13 with 1 Corinthians 14:35, and what Priscilla did in Acts 18:24-26 with 1 Timothy 2:11-12. What does this have to do with the way we interpret the prescriptions found in the New Testament?

2. How would you apply the principles of biblical interpretation that have been presented in this study to the discussion regarding homosexuality in the church? How would you apply them to other ethical questions alluded to in this chapter?

3. From your own experience, why is it so important to listen to people and be in dialogue with them when ethical decisions that affect them personally are being made?

4. What suggestions would you have for applying the "spirit" of the sabbath commandment and Jubilee laws today?

5. What dangers exist in insisting that one must deny oneself and love others *more* than oneself? How is it possible to keep a proper balance between loving others and loving yourself?

6. How has the material presented in this book changed your perspective on the interpretation of Scripture and its application to the questions and issues we face today as individuals, churches, and societies?

Bibliography

Banks, Robert J. 1975. *Jesus and the Law in the Synoptic Tradition.* Society for Old Testament Study Monograph Series 28. Cambridge: Cambridge University Press.

Childs, Jr., James M., ed. 2003. *Faithful Conversation: Christian Perspectives on Homosexuality.* Minneapolis: Fortress Press.

Davies, W. D. 1965. *Paul and Rabbinic Judaism: Some Rabbinic Elements in Pauline Theology.* 2nd ed. London: SPCK.

Dunn, James D. G. 1990. *Jesus, Paul and the Law: Studies in Mark and Galatians.* London: SPCK.

Hays, Richard B. 1996. *The Moral Vision of the New Testament: Community, Cross, New Creation: A Contemporary Introduction to New Testament Ethics.* San Francisco: HarperSanFrancisco.

Holwerda, David E. 1995. *Jesus & Israel: One Covenant or Two?* Grand Rapids, Mich.: Wm. B. Eerdmans.

Instone-Brewer, David. 2002. *Divorce and Remarriage in the Bible: The Social and Literary Context.* Grand Rapids, Mich.: Wm. B. Eerdmans.

Johnson, Luke Timothy. 1996. *Scripture and Discernment: Decision Making in the Church.* Nashville: Abingdon Press.

Neusner, Jacob. 1991. *The Talmud: A Close Encounter.* Minneapolis: Fortress Press.

Overman, J. Andrew. 1990. *Matthew's Gospel and Formative Judaism: The Social World of the Matthean Community.* Minneapolis: Fortress Press.

Pancaro, Severino. 1975. *The Law in the Fourth Gospel: The Torah and the Gospel, Moses and Jesus, Judaism and Christianity According to John.* Supplements to Novum Testamentum 42. Leiden: E. J. Brill.

Reventlow, Henning Graf and Yair Hoffman, eds. 1992. *Justice and Righteousness: Biblical Themes and Their Influence.* Journal for the Study of the Old Testament, Supplement Series 137. Sheffield: Sheffield Academic Press.

Ringe, Sharon H. 1985. *Jesus, Liberation, and the Biblical Jubilee: Images for Ethics and Christology.* Philadelphia: Fortress Press.

Sanders, E. P. 1977. *Paul and Palestinian Judaism.* Philadelphia: Fortress Press.

Notes

Chapter 1

1. On these points, see the following passages from the Talmud: *t.Shabbat* 16:22; *Shabbat* 36b; *Betzah* 9a.

2. *Genesis Rabbah* 1:4; 8:2, quoted in Jacob Neusner, *Torah: From Scroll to Symbol in Formative Judaism* (Philadelphia: Fortress Press, 1985), 119.

3. Werner Foerster, *Palestinian Judaism in New Testament Times*, trans. Gordon E. Harris (Edinburgh: Oliver and Boyd, 1964), 184–86.

4. E. P. Sanders, *Judaism: Practice and Belief 63 B.C.E.–66 C.E.* (Philadelphia: Trinity Press International, 1992), 467; cf. 123–24.

5. George A. F. Knight, *A Christian Theology of the Old Testament* (Richmond: John Knox Press, 1959), 250-53.

6. Georg Fohrer, *History of Israelite Religion*, trans. David E. Green (London: SPCK, 1972), 315.

Chapter 2

1. Among the many works discussing Jesus' understanding of the Law, the following may be mentioned, all of which serve as the basis for much of the content in this chapter: William R. G. Loader, *Jesus' Attitude towards the Law: A Study of the Gospels* (Tübingen: J.C.B. Mohr, 1997); E. P. Sanders, *Jesus and Judaism* (Philadelphia: Fortress Press, 1985); Marcus J. Borg, *Conflict, Holiness, and Politics in the Teachings of Jesus* (Harrisburg, Pa.: Trinity Press International, 1998); Geza Vermes, *The Religion of Jesus the Jew* (Minneapolis: Fortress Press, 1993); Irving M. Zeitlin, *Jesus and the Judaism of His*

Time (Oxford: Basil Blackwell, 1988). These last two works are by Jewish scholars.

2. E. P. Sanders has particularly argued for the need to rethink our view of the Pharisees; on this point and what follows, see *Jesus and Judaism*, 270–93.

3. See Kim Huat Tan, *The Zion Tradition and the Aims of Jesus,* Society for New Testament Studies Monograph Series 91 (Cambridge: Cambridge University Press, 1997), 231–32.

4. See Amy-Jill Levine, "Matthew," in *Women's Bible Commentary*, Expanded Edition with Apocrypha, Carol A. Newsom and Sharon H. Ringe, eds. (Louisville: Westminster John Knox Press, 1998), 342.

Chapter 3

1. E. P. Sanders, *The Historical Figure of Jesus* (London: Penguin, 1995), 238.

2. On this point and what follows, see Ben Witherington III, *The Christology of Jesus* (Minneapolis: Fortress Press, 1990), 65.

3. See James D. G. Dunn, *Jesus Remembered*, vol. 1 of *Christianity in the Making* (Grand Rapids, Mich.: Wm. B. Eerdmans, 2003), 787–88.

4. See N. T. Wright, *Jesus and the Victory of God*, vol. 2 of *Christian Origins and the Question of God* (Minneapolis: Fortress Press, 1996), 647.

5. On this point, see Wright, *Jesus and the Victory of God*, 191–92.

6. See Mark Allan Powell, "Binding and Loosing: Asserting the Moral Authority of Scripture in Light of a Matthean Paradigm," *Ex Auditu* 19 (2003), 81–96.

7. Susanne Lehne discusses extensively the background of the concept of new covenant and its usage in the Christian Scriptures in *The New Covenant in Hebrews,* Journal for the Study of the New Testament Supplement Series 44, ed. David Hill (Sheffield: Sheffield Academic Press, 1990).

Chapter 4

1. On Paul's knowledge and use of Jesus' teaching on the Law, see especially David Wenham, *Paul: Follower of Jesus or Founder of Christianity?* (Grand Rapids, Mich.: Wm. B. Eerdmans, 1995), 215–241; Michael B. Thompson, *Clothed with Christ: The Example and Teaching of Jesus in Romans 12.1–15.13,* Journal for the Study of the New Testament Supplement Series 59 (Sheffield: JSOT Press, 1991), 121–40.

2. See John M. G. Barclay, *Obeying the Truth: A Study of Paul's Ethics in Galatians* (Edinburgh: T & T Clark, 1988), 125–45; James D. G. Dunn, *The Theology of Paul the Apostle* (Grand Rapids, Mich.: Wm. B. Eerdmans, 1998), 654–58.

3. On the background of this problem and Paul's discussion of it in 1 Corinthians 8 and 10, see Gerd Thiessen, *The Social Setting of Pauline Christianity: Essays on Corinth* (Philadelphia: Fortress Press, 1982), 121–43.

4. See Nikolaus Walter, "Paul and the Early Christian Jesus-Tradition," in Alexander J. M. Wedderburn, ed., *Paul and Jesus: Collected Essays* (Sheffield: Sheffield Academic Press, 1989), 68–74; Peter J. Tomson, "Paul's Jewish Background in View of His Law Teaching in 1 Cor 7," in James D. G. Dunn, ed., *Paul and the Mosaic Law: The Third Durham Tübingen Research Symposium on Earliest Christianity and Judaism* (Tübingen: J. C. B. Mohr, 1996), 264.

Chapter 6

1. See E. Elizabeth Johnson, "Colossians," in *Women's Bible Commentary*, 438.

2. A variety of perspectives on this issue, as well as a consideration of the relevant biblical texts, can be found in Arland J. Hultgren and Walter F. Taylor Jr., *Background Essay on Biblical Texts for "Journey Together Faithfully, Part Two: The Church and*

Homosexuality" (Chicago: Evangelical Lutheran Church in America, 2003).

3. The Evangelical Lutheran Church in America in particular has carried out studies and developed statements on a number of these issues. These can be obtained from the ELCA's Division for Church in Society.

4. On the subject of how the principle behind the biblical commandment regarding sabbath rest can be applied today by Christians, see the articles in *Interpretation* 59, no. 4 (January 2005).

5. For Jewish and Christian views regarding the application of the Jubilee laws today, see Hans Ucko, ed., *The Jubilee Challenge— Utopia or Possibility? Jewish and Christian Insights* (Geneva: WCC Publications, 1997).

Other Books from the Lutheran Voices Series

Will I Sing Again? by John McCullough Bade
96 pages, 0-8066-4998-4

Author John McCullough Bade reflects on his personal struggle with Parkinson's Disease, expressing his journey in startling poetry and prose.

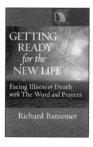

Getting Ready for the New Life by Richard Bansemer
96 pages, 0-8066-4988-7

Author Richard Bansemer provides comfort and encouragement for those facing illness and death, and for those who care for them, through Scriptural texts, reflections, and prayers.

Listen! God Is Calling by D. Michael Bennethum
96 pages, 0-8066-4991-7

Author D. Michael Bennethum presents Martin Luther's teaching on vocation as a resource both for individual believers and for congregations. Bennethum guides readers to listen for God's call in every aspect of life.

Other Books from the Lutheran Voices Series

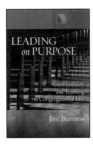

Leading on Purpose by Eric Burtness
96 pages, 0-8066-5174-1

Exploring the Purpose-Driven Church phenomenon, Eric Burtness provides pastors and church leaders with a Lutheran view of what it means to lead on purpose and integrates the Purpose-Driven philosophy into the context of Lutheran congregational life.

On a Wing and a Prayer by Michael Cooper-White
96 pages, 0-8066-4992-5

Uses the language of aviation to look at the principles of leadership and apply them to congregations and other organizations. The book also will encourage lay readers to consider how these principles can shape their daily lives and arenas where they live their Christian vocations.

Let the Servant Church Arise!
by Barbara DeGrote-Sorensen
and David Allen Sorensen
96 pages, 0-8066-4995-X

Authors Barbara DeGrote-Sorensen and David Allen Sorensen explore all aspects of Christian servanthood and how it can have a profound effect on both church and civil communities.

Other Books from the Lutheran Voices Series

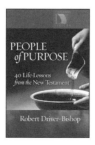

People of Purpose by Robert Driver-Bishop
112 pages, 0-8066-4936-4

The book explores forty New Testament people and the themes that emerge from their stories. Helps readers grow and mature in the faith by engaging in these themes from a "purpose" perspective.

Our Lives Are Not Our Own
by Rochelle Melander and Harold Eppley
96 pages, 0-8066-4999-2

Authors Rochelle Melander and Harold Eppley encourage personal reflective and creative dialogue about Christian accountability for the use of our lives, possessions, and abilities.

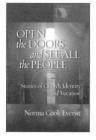

Open the Doors and See All the People
by Norma Cook Everist
112 pages, 0-8066-5161-X

Emerging from the author's interviews and interactions with numerous Lutheran congregations across the country, this book explores how congregations are determining and living out their identity.

Other Books from the Lutheran Voices Series

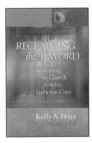

Reclaiming the "L" Word by Kelly A. Fryer
112 pages, 0-8066-4596-2

Inspirational, engaging, and challenging, author Kelly A. Fryer sets forth five Guiding Principles to ignite the church in a book that is a must-read for pastors and congregational leaders!

Water from the Rock by Ann E. Hafften
96 pages, 0-8066-4989-5

Contributing editor Ann E. Hafften provides articles, commentary, and stories from prominent Lutherans living in the strife-torn land of Palestine.

Who Do You Say That I Am? by Susan K. Hedahl
96 pages, 0-8066-4990-9

Author Susan K. Hedahl provides some basic definitions of preaching in the post-modern age and invites readers into a Holy encounter with Jesus through Lutheran preaching.

Other Books from the Lutheran Voices Series

Signs of Belonging by Mary E. Hinkle
96 pages, 0-8066-4997-6

Author Mary E. Hinkle explores Luther's teaching on the seven marks of the church, drawing the reader into a personal, spiritual exploration in dialogue with biblical wisdom.

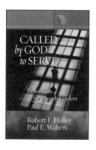

Called by God to Serve
by Robert F. Holley & Paul E. Walters
96 pages, 0-8066-5172-5

Church councils and leadership groups will discover ten helpful devotional reflections and discussion starters for a three-year cycle, focusing on the task of serving from a biblical and theological perspective.

Speaking of Trust by Martin E. Marty
160 pages, 0-8066-4994-1

Author Martin E. Marty brings together passages from Luther's preaching on the Sermon on the Mount and his own comments about the place of trust in the life of faith.

Other Books from the Lutheran Voices Series

Public Church by Cynthia Moe-Lobeda
112 pages, 0-8066-4987-9

The Evangelical Lutheran Church in America professes to be a public church constituted by God for its public vocation. Moe-Lobeda explores what it means for the ELCA to play a role in public life today.

Connecting with God in a Disconnected World
by Carolyn Coon Mowchan
and Damian Anthony Vraniak.
96 pages, 0-8066-4996-8

Authors Carolyn Coon Mowchan and Damian Anthony Vraniak encourage adult readers to examine the barriers that keep us from experiencing a more full relationship with God.

Give Us This Day by Craig L. Nessan
96 pages, 0-8066-4993-3

Author Craig L. Nessan summons the Christian church to listen to the cries of the hungry and commit itself to ending hunger as a matter of *status confessionis.*

Other Books from the Lutheran Voices Series

LUTHERAN
VOICES

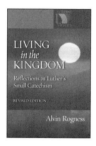

Living in the Kingdom by Alvin Rogness
112 pages, 0-8066-4934-8

This revised and updated classic by beloved theologian Alvin N. Rogness explores questions like, "What does it mean to be a responsible citizen of God's kingdom? And how do the teachings of the Bible and the church help us meet the often perplexing problems of life?"

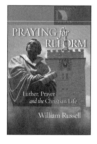

Praying for Reform by William Russell
96 pages, 0-8066-5111-3

A Lutheran scholar explores how prayer shaped Luther's life and informed his writing and teaching. From Luther's life of prayer emerges his emphasis on Catechesis—teaching the basics of Christian faith and practice.

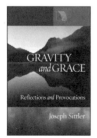

Gravity and Grace by Joseph Sittler
128 pages, 0-8066-5173-3

This newly revised edition provides insights from one of the leading Lutheran theologians of the twentieth century. The essays and reflections gathered in this volume provoke readers to think about and discuss topics such as risk and faith, nature and grace, the Word of God, and genuine theology.